There is no cure for birth and death save to enjoy the interval.
— Santayana

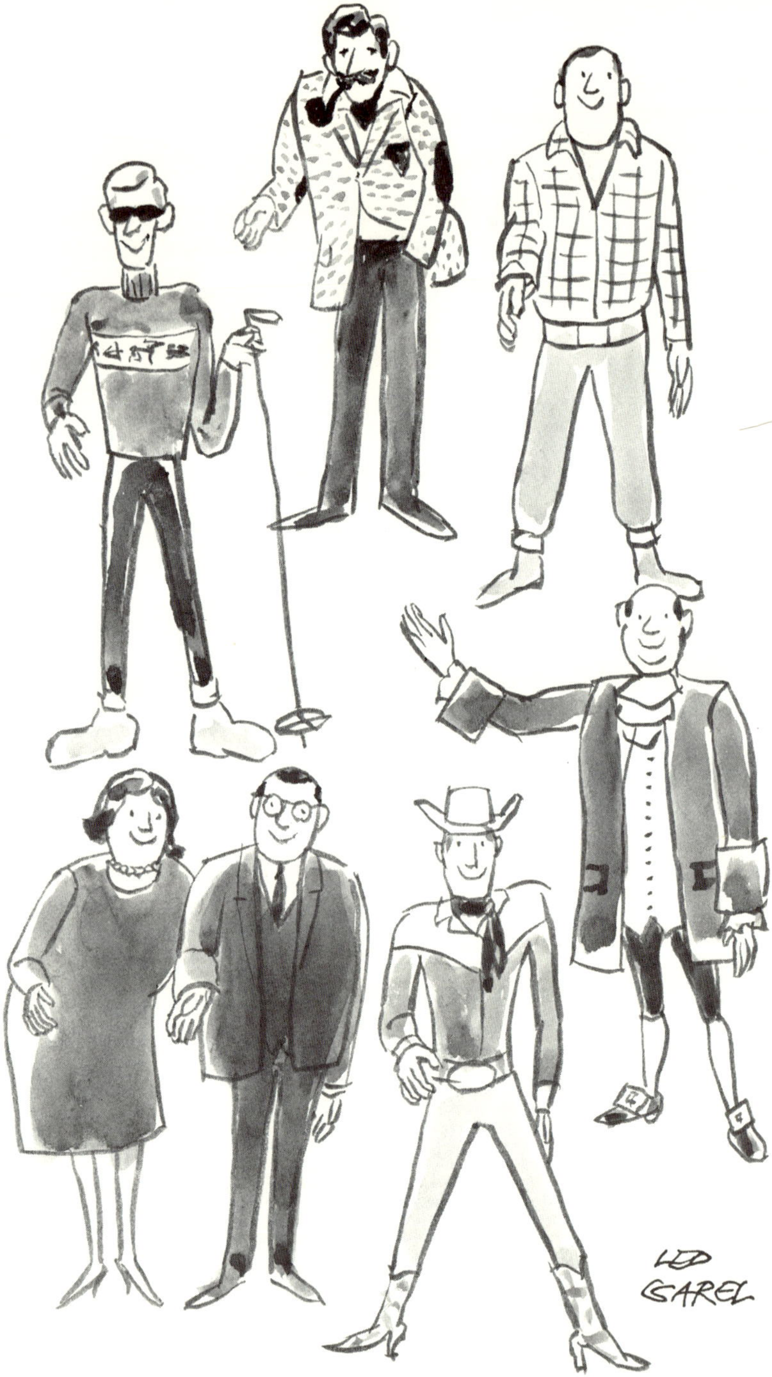
LEO
GAREL

How to Open a
COUNTRY INN

Karen L. Etsell
in collaboration with
Elaine C. Brennan

●

Illustrations by **Leo Garel**

THE BERKSHIRE TRAVELLER PRESS
Stockbridge, Massachusetts

SELECTED TITLES FROM BERKSHIRE TRAVELLER PRESS

Country Inns and Back Roads, North America
Country Inns and Back Roads, Britain and Ireland
Country Inns and Back Roads, Europe
Country Inns and Back Roads Cookbook
Bed & Breakfast, American Style
A Guide to Music Festivals in America
Music Festivals in Europe
Country Bed and Breakfast Places in Canada
Austria . . . The Inn Way
The Bahamas . . . The Inn Way
The Caribbean . . . The Inn Way
Switzerland . . . The Inn Way
Home Landscaping
Practical Plans for Barns
Measured Drawings of Shaker Furniture
Flea Market Handbook

Copyright © 1981 by Karen L. Etsell and Elaine C. Brennan All rights reserved. No part of this book may be used or reproduced in any manner whatsoever without written permission. For information address The Berkshire Traveller Press, Inc., Stockbridge, Massachusetts 01262

COVER PAINTING: Alice Young
ILLUSTRATIONS: Leo Garel

ISBN 0-912-94469-2
Library of Congress No. 81-67696

Printed in the United States of America by The Studley Press, Inc., Dalton, Massachusetts 01226

6 5 4 3

To Jerry

CONTENTS

Foreword	11
Preface	15
Acknowledgments	18

PART I — ON BECOMING AN INNKEEPER

What is a Country Inn, Anyway?	21
1 The "Dream" and the "Need"	23
2 Your Dream Versus Your Pocketbook	30
Getting Down to Brass Tacks	31
Real Estate as a Business Investment	32
3 Advance Preparations	34
Preliminary Study	35
4 Looking for the Right Place for You	40
Searching for the Right Location	42
Narrowing Your Search	45
The Perils of a Seasonal Business	49

CONTENTS

5	Determining Who Will be Your Clientele	53
	Why Will the Public Choose to Visit Your Country Inn	53
	To Have or Not to Have a Dining Room	57
	Personality Profile of a Country Innkeeper	59

PART II — GETTING YOUR INN READY TO OPEN

6	The Business Side of Innkeeping	63
	How to Get Financing for Your Country Inn	63
	The Use of Professional Consultants	65
	Forms of Business Ownership	66
	Licensing	68
	A Pro Forma Analysis	72
7	On Running a Restaurant	77
	Can You Succeed When Others Fail?	78
	What to Cook	79
	How Much to Cook	82
	Hire a Chef or Do It Yourself?	82
	How Large Will Your Restaurant Be?	84
	Cost and Profit Margins	84
	"Freebies"	86
	The Restaurant Business as Live Theater	87
8	Establishing the Theme or Style of Your Inn	89
	Redecorating	92
	Furnishing Your Inn	95

Contents

9	Purchasing for Your Inn	97
	Equipment and Supplies	97
	Basic Shopping List	99
	Food Purchasing	106
	Wine and Beer Purchasing	107
	Purchasing Tips	108
10	Personnel	109
	The Organization of Personnel	110
	The Omnipresent Innkeeper	112
11	Getting Your Story Told	114
	Advertising	115
	Publicity	123
	Promotion	128

PART III — OPERATING A SUCCESSFUL COUNTRY INN

12	Basic Operating Procedures	137
	Innkeeper-Guest Relations	138
	Maintaining Your Inn	146
13	Expansion and Growth	150
	Capitalize on Your Theme	150
	How Will You Grow?	155
	How Do You Judge Success?	156

Epilogue: One Day in the Life of a Country Innkeeper — 158

Index — 161

FOREWORD

For quite a few years I have had an increasingly urgent feeling that with the rapidly growing interest in owning country inns (if my mail on the subject is any indicator) a book on the subject would be most helpful in guiding enthusiastic prospective innkeepers. Further, as a result of many meetings with people who entertained the idea of becoming innkeepers, I found that one of their principal assets was an enthusiasm that was frequently misguided: "Well, we've always liked people, and my wife and I enjoy giving parties—she is a very good cook!" was the comment typical of the man in the case. The dialogue usually went one step farther, "We thought we would sell our house and use the net profit as a down payment on an inn in the country and start a whole new way of life."

I would explain that innkeeping involved much more than being a genial host and being able to stage a successful dinner party. One must have good business management skills as well as being able to fill in at any task.

Some people suggested that I write a book about how to open a country inn, but I felt that only someone who had actually started an inn within the last ten years would have the necessary experiences and qualifications to proffer such advice.

That's why I was so happy to hear from Karen Etsell and Elaine Brennan, two active, successful innkeepers, that they were writing just such a book and they were kind enough to offer me two opportunities: one, to publish it, and two, to write a foreword.

I had visited them at The Bramble Inn in Brewster on the north shore of Cape Cod a few years ago and was struck not only by the originality of their efforts, but also by their extremely businesslike approach to the enterprise. As you will learn, they went to a great deal of trouble to spell out their objectives and to set goals long before even visiting the Cape. I've included their inn in *Country Inns and Back Roads, North America* every year since 1977 and have been applauding their increasing success.

As soon as I read the first few chapters of their manuscript and saw the outline for the remainder of the book, I knew that this was exactly what I'd been looking for to fill the need for information on opening and operating a country inn. In the first place, it has been written by two innkeepers who are very actively involved in their inn and seeking new solutions to new problems. They are not willing to sit back and "rest on their laurels," they're seeing new opportunities almost every day.

Karen and Elaine possess most of the built-in attributes that every innkeeper should have: they are flexible, imaginative, hard-working, and were successful in other fields before going into innkeeping.

Another feature that makes this book an important contribution to innkeeping is the fact that the authors are not only innkeepers but also women. I say this because as a result of conversations with women innkeepers all over North America, Britain, and Europe, I'm convinced that women have many inherent qualities that make them wonderfully qualified for innkeeping. Furthermore, an increasing number of women are proving to be extremely adept at the "behind the scenes" aspects of innkeeping—dealing with real estate agents, bankers, builders, plumbers, electricians, carpenters, and meat and produce suppliers.

The authors are not dilettante innkeepers merely bent on having a lark. Their approach is pragmatic, and from the very outset they share with the reader some of the difficulties that any new innkeeper would encounter. The book is a primer for entering the field of innkeeping today.

If ever you've had the pleasant urge to operate a country inn, I hope you'll read this book carefully from cover to cover. Not only is it a wonderfully comprehensive look at innkeeping, including almost all of the nuts and bolts, but it also provides some guidelines by which to examine your own dreams and to see in reality whether or not this is a valid adventure for you.

Norman T. Simpson

PREFACE

Ah! The idyllic life of a country innkeeper! So many people have dreams of someday owning a lovely country inn far away from the demands of this hectic world.

"How did *you* become a country innkeeper?" they ask. I cannot count the number of times my partner Elaine and I have been asked this question during the past six years. We receive long letters of inquiry with detailed questions; guests stop us in the hallways and in the dining rooms and want to discuss the vicissitudes of innkeeping; people ask if they can come to the inn and follow us around for a week or so to get the "feel" of innkeeping. And my fellow innkeeper friends report the same phenomenon.

Frequently, in conversation, it is clear that the person is really asking, "How can *I* become a country innkeeper? Would I like it? Could I open my own inn, too?" They envision a slower-paced life style in a bucolic setting with interesting people to keep them company. They dream of a place where they can be independent, creative, and peaceful— a place where they can live in financial comfort and security enjoying the genteel pleasures of life.

Having been a country innkeeper for six years, I can say that much of this picture is true—sometimes! But, for much of the time, being an innkeeper is far from the peaceful, idyllic scenario just described. Owning an inn is a business, and just like any other business, it is filled with many of the same problems, heartaches, joys, anxieties, challenges, and rewards.

There is indeed great joy in creating your own independent way of life. There is the pleasure of seeing people truly enjoy themselves in an environment you have created for them. Just yesterday a woman told me that she and her husband had had one of the very best times *of their lives* at The Bramble Inn. Hearing that kind of satisfaction makes all one's efforts worthwhile. The joy is probably never more intense than on that day when you finally hang your sign in front of your inn, opening the door to the public for the first time. Only you can experience that flood of pride in your accomplishment, knowing all the determination and hard work it took to get to Opening Day!

But what about the despair that assails you the next week after opening day when absolutely no one is registered in the inn and not a soul comes for lunch except your major local competitors? Embarrassment, frustration, discomfort, anger, sadness—all these emotions line up right after DESPAIR! Six years later, however, when business is booming your joy is even greater because of all the pangs you suffered during the slow days of building your business.

Despair is also close to what you feel when you realize on Sunday night of the Fourth of July weekend that no hot water is coming out of your commercial hot water heater, and your supplier says it will be three to four days at the earliest before he can get you a new one. How will your guests take showers? How will your dining room dishes get washed? How will you do the laundry? Being an innkeeper teaches you a great deal of resourcefulness; there is *always* a solution to even the greatest problem. Luckily, we remembered that the previous owner had left a small residential hot water heater which we could hook up in an emergency. The supply of hot water was not plentiful, but we managed. The guests showered first, we did cold water laundry washes, and we washed dishes in small batches till the new hot water heater was finally installed.

Murphy's Law was undoubtedly written by an innkeeper: "If there is a possibility that something can go wrong, the chances are very good that it will." It is amazing how major pieces of equipment wait till weekends to fail when there is no service available. We have had our oven break down on Friday night and we had to serve everything from the top of the stove for the entire weekend.

Innkeeping teaches you to have a good sense of humor, too—particularly when dealing with guests. We spend a lot of time and effort on developing and perfecting our recipes, and we are particularly proud of some of our delicate crepe recipes which people love. One night a man requested hot Tabasco sauce for his chicken crêpes élégante. Although the waitress was dubious, she did bring him the hot sauce. On leaving, the man exclaimed on how delicious the crepes were and assured us he was certainly going to send his wife over soon to try them. Sure enough, within the week, a woman came and ordered chicken crepes which had been highly recommended by her husband. She thought they were terrific, too—especially after she added the Tabasco hot sauce to them! As I said, a sense of humor does help.

An embarrassing moment in our innkeeping history occurred one night around nine o'clock when a guest came to the front desk and sheepishly asked if he could borrow a broom and dustpan to sweep up some ceiling plaster that had just fallen! A portion of the ceiling had collapsed! We had noticed a slight crack, but it hadn't seemed to warrant any immediate repair. Luckily, no one was injured and the guests, who had stayed with us before, were quite unruffled by the incident. We hoped that the complimentary wine we sent up to their room helped them rest comfortably that night, without fear that the rest of the sky would fall in on them. Luckily, we were able to have the ceiling repaired the very next day.

These true-life experiences begin to suggest that "idyllic" may not be the most accurate adjective to use in describing the life of an innkeeper! It is, however, a life filled with stimulation, challenges, beauty, creativity, and many, many rewards.

The purpose of writing this book is to share the knowledge and experiences we have accumulated during our years as innkeepers and to reveal both the joys and the warts of innkeeping. If you still dream about becoming an innkeeper, I hope the rest of this book will assist you in attaining your dream.

ACKNOWLEDGMENTS

We want to thank Alice and Jack Brennan for all their advice and encouragement, especially during the initial stages of developing The Bramble Inn, and for their belief in us. We thank Country Business Services and the many innkeepers who have contributed to this book by generously sharing their experiences. We thank Virginia Rowe who edited the manuscript so skillfully. And, finally, we thank Norman Simpson for his continued support and promotion of the spirit of country innkeeping.

PART I

On Becoming An Innkeeper

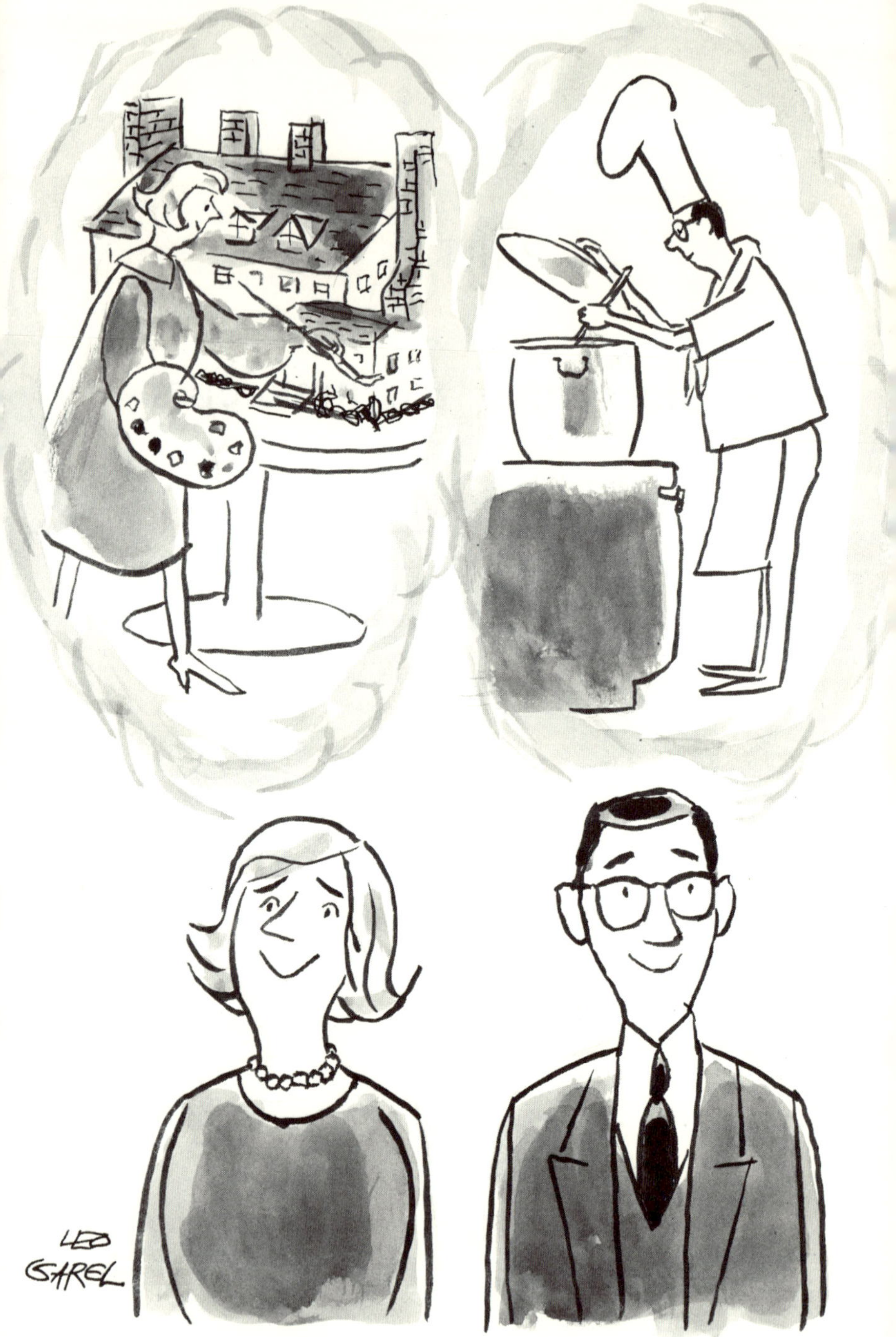
LEO GAREL

WHAT IS A COUNTRY INN, ANYWAY?

Before taking up the question of becoming a country innkeeper, we should define just what a country inn is. Arriving at a definition is difficult even for someone who has run a country inn for six years. There are many common characteristics, and many more uncommon ones. For example, a number of country inns are located in older, historically significant buildings, but there are also country inns which are wholly or in part newly built structures.

Traditionally, country inns provide both lodging and dining facilities; however, there are some inns that are only restaurants with no lodging facilities at all. Some country inns provide lodging accommodations and no dining facilities (with the usual exception of a continental breakfast to start the traveler on his way). Well, you say, at least a country inn has to be located in the country. Why, then, does Norman Simpson, author of the well-known Country Inns and Back Roads, *include in his book The Algonquin Hotel in Manhattan, New York, as well as the Jefferson Hotel in Washington, D.C., the Bed and Breakfast Inn and the Union Street Hotel in San Francisco, and the Brazilian Court in Palm Beach? Are there no basic, shared, common characteristics of this entity called a country inn?*

Our belief is that all country inns do have one basic quality which is at the heart of the matter. A country inn is a distinctive, personal statement of the identity, style, and taste of the innkeeper. The inn is really an expression of the innkeeper's personality, *and if the many facets of the inn blend successfully with the innkeeper's personality, then the inn is a success. If the innkeeper is not true to himself, then the inn is without a sense of harmony and balance, which is reflected in all aspects of its operation and, in turn, is not pleasing to the guests.*

A country inn, then, is not defined by the number of old working fireplaces, or the age of the wide pine floorboards, or by the presence of lodging or dining rooms. It is defined by its innkeeper, who presents a warm, hospitable, highy individual, and gracious ambience for people to "BE." Quite a difference from the plastic repetition of commercial lodgings! By spending time in an environment which is a strong statement of personal identity and preference, guests are encouraged to relax in the comfort of their own *personalities. There is an old adage that says, "A life well lived is the best revenge." Somehow, every innkeeper is able to transmit to his guests the message that spending time at his inn is a part of a "life well lived."*

Lastly, country inns share one other important characteristic. They are places where the guest has the feeling of being a person *rather than a room number, and where the first and foremost concern is the comfort of the guest. A country inn is a place where there is an atmosphere of personal interest which conveys a sense of friendly conviviality. Although the best country inns have their own distinctive signatures, there are many that provide simple comfort and cleanliness in homey surroundings, whose major distinction is making their guests feel welcome and well cared for. The key point in all cases is* personal involvement.

1
THE "DREAM" AND THE "NEED"

There are two fundamental requirements for becoming a successful innkeeper: you must have both the "Dream" and the "Need" to undertake such a project. The "Dream" might come to you one morning while taking a shower in Los Angeles as it did to me. Or, you may have always wanted to own a guest house on Cape Cod from early childhood. However you achieve it, the "Dream" is a *sine qua non* for getting you over all the hurdles that you will encounter during your innkeeping years. If you lose sight of your "Dream"—of what you are personally trying to accomplish—then your innkeeping venture will become shaky and vulnerable.

The "Need," on the other hand, is often more complex than the "Dream." Whereas the "Dream" is usually born of single-mindedness and oneness of purpose, the "Need" has both psychological and economic components motivated by personal and social goals.

Some people choose innkeeping in order to become independent, to be his or her own boss, or to establish a nest egg. Conversely, others choose innkeeping because they are already independently wealthy, enjoy entertaining, and feel that innkeeping would be a way of fulfilling their need to meet new and interesting people.

Innkeeping can be viewed as a way to keep families together by having a common purpose, and this has proven to be extremely successful for a number of inns. Our neighbors on the Cape, Ted and Marce Barker have not only immediate members of their family, but also the new wives and husbands of their sons and daughters, involved in the operation of their Red Inn in Provincetown. At the Lowell Inn in Minnesota, Arthur and Maureen Palmer have been employing their large family of children continually in all of the diverse duties of the inn. Arthur's father and mother actually started the Lowell Inn and Arthur grew up there. All of the four McMahon children pitch in at the Inn at Starlight Lake in Pennsylvania.

An increased sense of family closeness develops in situations of mutual interdependence—not to mention the actual physical closeness of working together with spouse or children for sixteen to eighteen hours a day. And the experience is often of great benefit to the children, helping them to develop self-reliance and a sense of responsibility, as well as providing a later possible career choice. Again, there are a multitude of examples where children of innkeepers have chosen to remain in the business: for instance, the Beaumont Inn in Kentucky has had four generations of innkeepers, and a possible fifth generation has just recently arrived. Frank Whitman is a second-generation innkeeper at the family-run Silvermine Tavern in Connecticut. John Stone is now the innkeeper at the Captain Whidbey Inn in Washington which was started by his mother and father, Shirlie and Steve Stone; Johnny Edge and his sister Betsi grew up at the Rockhouse Mountain Farm in New Hampshire, and even though Betsi is now married, she is the chief cook and Johnny is in charge of all of the outside activities and the grounds. Gordon Shaw spent his boyhood at the family-owned Shaw's Hotel on Prince Edward Island, and is now the general manager there; the same is true of Scott

The "Dream" and the "Need"

MacAulay at the Inverary Inn in Nova Scotia. At the Inn at Sawmill Farm in Vermont, Brill Williams learned from his mother how to cook, and is now the head chef and one of the owners. And there are many more examples of total family involvement in innkeeping.

There is a growing phenomenon lately of more and more "Mom and Pop" businesses developing because people want to reduce the isolation and alienation which they often feel in their work world. The growing popularity of innkeeping certainly attests to this trend. Innkeeping can provide an alternate life style of quieter country living to those who seek refuge from the hassles of city living. (Unless, of course, you own a "country inn" in the middle of a metropolis.)

For people with broad creative talents, innkeeping offers a stage for displaying a wide range of talents for cooking, interior design, architecture, and landscaping, as well as creative personnel management, advertising, promotion, and financial planning. I can think of several cases where an interesting combination of talents has surfaced among various innkeepers. At Schumacher's New Prague Hotel in Minnesota, John is the chef and Nancy has completely redesigned the interior of the inn with wonderful central European touches. While Bob Lenz's talents at the Asa Ransom House in Clarence, New York, run toward organization and administration, his wife Judy has proven to be a whiz at designing and decorating the really outstanding lodging rooms at their small inn. Both Orville and Audrey Orr at the Buxton Inn in Ohio were schoolteachers for many years until they discovered a talent for restoring, decorating, and furnishing their truly handsome 1812 inn. Hours of research and study inspired Kelley and Ashby Berkley to create the ambience of 1607 Jamestown, Virginia, in their Riverside Inn in West Virginia.

The "Need," therefore, can be as broad as the spectrum of people who choose to become innkeepers. Of particular note in this spectrum of prospective innkeepers are those individuals seeking a second career as a way out of what is commonly referred to as the "rat race." Many people who have made a successful career in professional or corporate circles find, in their mid-lives, an urge to return to the simpler virtues of a quieter life style. Typically, these people have some business, management, or perhaps advertising background which makes opening their own business a likely choice. Especially if someone likes to cook and/or eat, the prospect of starting a little gourmet restaurant along with the inn seems a natural conclusion. The country inn life begins to sound just like Nirvana!

Many successful innkeepers do come to the field in just this way, the primary "Need" being to get out of the rat race. Bob Hull was a corporate executive catching the commuter train every day from Fairfield County to New York City, when he and his wife Fran decided nine years ago to buy the Pine Crest Inn in the foothills of the Blue Ridge Mountains of North Carolina. Charles Schubert was a radio personality and his wife Marilyn was an airline stewardess before they started looking for a country inn over ten years ago—they found the Barrows House in the little town of Dorset, Vermont. And there are many similar stories.

For those who are trying to get out of the rat race, becoming an innkeeper can be a gratifying transition if you are well-prepared and stable. It can also be a huge disappointment for those who have unreasonable expectations of the joys of the "simpler, rural life." The change of pace from the stimulating, demanding city to the slower tempo of the country can present a difficult adjustment. Not that you will have too much time on your hands! More often, running a country inn presents an unexpectedly brisk pace of demands and frustrations peculiar to itself. Many of these demands are basic, unglamourous tasks having to do with providing service to your guests. In a small, family-run country inn—especially in the off-season—changing sheets and cleaning bathrooms may become the "rural rat race" activities of an innkeeper. There are certainly differences between the pressures of innkeeping and the city-paced corporate world, but no prospective innkeeper should minimize the stresses that must be met in this new career. (See "One Day in the Life of a Country Innkeeper," page 158.)

For people who have travelled extensively and observed the multitude of styles in which others provide hospitality, innkeeping can be a natural choice. It also helps to have the ability to make people feel comfortable, to be at ease with new situations and new acquaintances, and to be conversant with a wide area of interests.

Innkeeping can be the perfect career for someone who likes to work with his/her hands. Being skilled as a plumber, carpenter, electrician, wallpaper hanger, or painter comes in very handy as an innkeeper. If you enjoy tinkering or if your friends call you Mr. or Mrs. Fixit, you will find life as an innkeeper a delight!

I was not necessarily inclined to be a handy person a few years ago. But the many small things that go wrong and the high hourly service charges to repair even minor problems have sparked my interest in learning these necessary skills. One night before I had learned about repairing water faucet washers, the sink's tiny drip suddenly turned into a deluge. Not only did I not know how to repair the washer, I didn't even know that the shut-off valve was right under the sink. So the water continued to pour out relentlessly until a plumber could be called. Twenty-five dollars later, I decided I could learn to replace worn-out faucet washers! With a little reading (the *New York Times Manual of Home Repairs* is very helpful) and practice, I've even mastered O-rings, washers in the faucet seats, pop-up drain repairs, and minor toilet repairs as well. If you come to your innkeeping career already skilled in these areas, so much the better for you!

The successful innkeeper has a strong drive for independence and security, and he/she sees his/her inn as a stage for the pursuit of excellence. It helps to be a perfectionist and a seeker of quality. Having the chance to own one's own business is, after all, the American Dream. It's a great arrangement when "doing your own thing" is also doing your daily work. It can be likened to the joy of an artist or performer whose creative activity is also his life's work. When people share and appreciate and participate in his creation, the pleasure is great, indeed. There is also a vicarious pleasure that the innkeeper experiences: in providing the means by which others may enjoy themselves, some of the fun "rubs off" on the innkeeper. There is enormous therapeutic value in relaxation and pleasure, and the innkeeper is instrumental in providing this by helping people enjoy their leisure time. As an innkeeper you do have a positive impact on people and you have fun while you are making money (hopefully).

SOME "NEEDS" NOT RECOMMENDED FOR INNKEEPERS

There are some "Needs" which are contraindicated for innkeepers. If your marriage is rocky, chances are slight that owning an inn together with your spouse will *help* your relationship. It *will* bring you closer together. But there are many, many demands on your time, patience, and cooperative spirit which will probably drive the wedge deeper between you and split the relationship even more quickly. Innkeeping is not for those with unstable relationships; rather, it is for those who enjoy and work well together for long hours each day.

Neither is innkeeping for those who have a low tolerance for pressure or who seek solace in alcohol. The temptation to drink to relieve tension is great since alcohol is usually readily available in one's own lounge. This is a problem that no industry likes to focus on, but innkeeping is an entertainment business with many pressures and each person has to determine for himself how to deal with these pressures.

The "Dream" and the "Need"

Another related potential problem is overeating in your wonderful restaurant with all the delicious sauces, homebaked breads, and sweet desserts. During our first season, we thought that eating from the menu was a good quality control checking system. We both gained ten pounds in twelve weeks!

Poor eating habits also take the form of "eating on the run" and not taking time to eat properly. Each innkeeper sooner or later learns how to organize his mealtimes to assure good nutrition and health. Remember, if you get sick, usually there is no one to substitute for you. Innkeeping, therefore, is not a cure for those who are already succumbing to the pressures of life with symptoms of over-drinking and over-eating.

2
YOUR DREAM VERSUS YOUR POCKETBOOK

Before continuing further with your dream of becoming an innkeeper, perhaps it would be wise first to consider some of the hard, cold facts. Tailoring your dream of innkeeping to fit your needs may really mean tailoring your wishes to fit your pocketbook!

Research shows that fifty percent of all new businesses fail during the first two years. Two-thirds of all new businesses fail during the first five years. It usually takes three to five years in business before you can judge whether or not it will be a success. For a seasonal business, it takes even longer—usually seven to eight years to see if it really makes it. So, it is good to have long-range sights of at least five years when starting a business to give it adequate time to grow and flourish. Undercapitalization is the single most common reason for new businesses to fail. So always plan on the conservative side of income received and on the generous side for projected expenses.

Economic considerations help to determine some aspects of innkeeping such as the size and scope of the inn. The number of lodging rooms and the seating capacity of your dining room are frequently determined by how much

Dream Versus Pocketbook

money you have to invest in the operation of your inn. If you have limited funds, you can begin by operating a first-class, smaller inn and, then gradually you can expand into a larger operation. By then, you will have acquired more expertise and capital to invest in the project. However, a word of caution is in order here: always keep in mind the possibilities of future expansion of your inn when you are purchasing property. You must always plan for success. And when success does come as the fruit of your hard labor, you will naturally want to grow and expand in at least some aspects of your business.

GETTING DOWN TO BRASS TACKS

How much money do you need to open a country inn? The exact amount varies greatly with the size and scope of your inn. But there are some general guidelines you can follow. You will probably need twenty to thirty percent of the purchase price of the property available for the down payment. You can figure out what the annual carrying costs will be for interest, principal, and taxes given the current mortgage interest rates. In order to get your inn opened, you will need cash for a wide variety of expenses including renovations, restoration and repairs, landscaping, furnishings, signs, licenses, consultants, insurance (liability and fire), living expenses until the first receipts come in, as well as emergency reserves. A rough estimate of the amount of the "working capital" needed during this period would be fifteen to thirty percent of the down payment.

Using as an example an inn that costs $300,000, a 30% down payment would require $90,000 in cash, plus an additional $13,500 to $27,000 in working capital. On this same property, if you obtained a $210,000 mortgage for 25 years at a 15% interest rate, your monthly payment of principal and interest would be $2689.77. The best advice is to assume that you have planned too low for expenses. Considering the time it takes to establish a clientele, actual income usually turns out to be lower than even your minimal expectations. Conversely, expenses are frequently higher than your direst projections. In figuring income, Country Business Services maintains that an inn must aim for an annual minimum of at least $5,000 per room and $2,000 per seat in the restaurant in order to have a successful operation.

An expense which will begin immediately upon opening your country inn is your advertising budget. (See Chapter 11, "Advertising.") You can spend a great deal of money on advertising without even half trying. A good rule of thumb is to set aside roughly ten percent of your projected gross profit for your advertising campaign annually.

An expense which is of mounting concern to innkeepers during the past decade is relatively new. That is the ever-increasing cost of energy. Large, rambling old country inns were not built during the age of energy consciousness. Many have minimal or no insulation and even the process of making them energy-efficient is fraught with problems. For example, you can add insulation to the roof, but the walls are often too narrow to install much insulation. (Blown-in insulation seems to be the best solution in these cases.) So the cost of heating a country inn during the winter, especially in the northern states, becomes a major expense. Even the cost of providing hot water becomes a large operating cost that the new innkeeper should not underestimate.

REAL ESTATE AS A BUSINESS INVESTMENT

If you decide that you have enough cash to meet these various expenses and to forge ahead with your plans to buy a country inn, there is some good news along the way.

If you buy an older building in need of renovation, you are automatically engaged in the business of real estate development. This process will undoubtedly result in a remarkable appreciation in your real estate investment. Turning a former "white elephant" into a tastefully restored and usable building can be a real money-making venture. I know some innkeepers who felt that the return on their investment in real estate appreciation alone was financially worthwhile—even if the business of innkeeping did not succeed! Luckily for them, both areas have been financially rewarding!

I must add, however, that there is another school of thought that claims the high mortgage rates and, basically, the cost of financing property development in the existing market make this a venture of dubious profitability.

The real estate investment plays another major role in the business of innkeeping. Because of the nature of the business, innkeepers usually live on the inn's premises. They get to enjoy the charm and pleasures of living in a lovely setting—one that most people have to pay to enjoy on vacation only. Because the innkeeper lives at his place of business—for the convenience of the business—there are many tax advantages and business deductions which can increase the profitability of innkeeping. At least a portion of expenses such as utilities, repairs, travel, telephone, and so forth, are bona fide business expenses through which the innkeeper benefits by having his home and work in the same location. During the early lean years, when taxable income is minimal, an innkeeper can live very comfortably because of all these advantages built into the nature of the business.

3
ADVANCE PREPARATIONS

Some innkeepers have made an early career choice and have gained extensive education and training at a hotel school such as the Cornell School of Hotel Management, the Culinary Institute in Hyde Park, or in various other schools of hotel management offered by a number of colleges and universities. There are a number of country innkeepers who have followed that path: John Harney of the White Hart Inn in Connecticut, Murray Schuman of the Inn at Huntington in Massachusetts, Jack McWilliams at Gristmill Square in Virginia, and Bill North at The Country Inn in West Virginia.

Other people have worked in various capacities in hotels, inns, and restaurants and have learned their profession through on-the-job training, so to speak. Ken and Wendy Gibson worked for almost a year in a Montreal restaurant which helped them immeasurably when they became the innkeepers at the Robert Morris Inn in Maryland. Bob and Sue Crory worked for many years at a large resort in Maine before opening their own Country Club Inn in Maine, and Marc Donaldson was a chef at an inn in Vermont before he and Marily took over the Darby

Field Inn in New Hampshire. Janice and Stafford Smith had worked at Stafford's Bay View in Michigan—she as hostess and he as assistant manager—before they fell in love and were married and saved up the money to buy the inn.

Still other innkeepers have drawn from their training and experience in a very wide range of diverse backgrounds, including business, teaching, real estate, engineering, housekeeping, antique collecting, personnel management, social work, parenting, sales, and just about anything else you can think of. Theadora McBroom who, along with her husband Bruce, is the innkeeper at the Old Milano Hotel in California, has been a successful costume designer for films. In fact, she set a whole new fashion trend a few years ago with her costumes for *Bonny and Clyde*. The innkeepers of the Whitehall Inn in Maine, Ed and Jean Dewing, were in the advertising business in Boston until about ten years ago. Engineering was Jim Shipe's field until he and his wife Mary Jo and their four children migrated to the Pasquaney Inn on Newfound Lake in New Hampshire. Rod and Ione Williams have not entirely given up their architectural design business, and combine it with keeping their Inn at Sawmill Farm. A noted gourmet chef and for many years head of the drama department at the University of Washington, John Ashby Conway now concentrates on dazzling his guests at his beloved Farmhouse restaurant in Port Townsend. People combine their skills and knowledge in this "jack of all trades" profession called innkeeping.

PRELIMINARY STUDY

One of the very first things I did after deciding to open my own business was to attend a free one-day workshop given in Los Angeles by the Small Business Association (SBA) entitled "How to Open Your Own Business." This workshop presented an excellent overview of the wide areas of concern I would have as a successful small business person. Topics included Accounting, Legal

Matters, Advertising, Trade Associations, Government Regulations, Taxes, Insurance, Public Relations and Promotion, Types of Business Ownership, and Personnel Management. I had had previous executive level management experience in a non-profit human service organization and was already familiar with many of these areas. But they all took on a new level of significance for me when I realized they would determine the profit margin from the investment of my own dollar! Presentations were made by professionals in each field discussing their areas of expertise. By attending the workshop, I came to a very important realization—even beyond the specific information learned that day. I discovered that there was no mystique to running a successful business. There were no "secrets" to be learned; that good business practices and a lot of hard work usually account for success. Since I could manage both of these things, I figured there was no way I could lose! If you have no previous experience in business management, I would strongly recommend calling your local SBA office to find out where and when the next workshop on "How to Open Your Own Business" will be held.

The SBA also issues an extensive list of free and low-cost publications designed for owner-managers and prospective owners of small businesses. I was particularly interested in reading *Starting and Managing a Small Business of Your Own* and *Starting and Managing a Small Restaurant,* as well as a number of management-aid manuals ranging from "Accounting Procedures" to "Zeal in Marketing." I have included a list of publications that will be helpful. If you want to inquire for new publications, a free list of available publications can be obtained by writing SBA, Washington, D.C., or any SBA's field offices. Ask for: "Free Management Assistance Publications" (SBA-115A) and "For-Sale Booklets" (SBA-115B). The information available in these publications is invaluable to a new business person—like taking a refresher course (or a crash

Advance Preparations

course!) in business administration. I still refer to the brochures from time to time and always find some new and relevant information.

Here is a list of management assistance leaflets available through any office of the Small Business Administration.

MANAGEMENT AIDS (free)

#32	How Trade Associations Help Small Businesses
#46	How to Analyze Your Own Business
#52	Loan Sources in the Federal Government
#80	Choosing the Legal Structure for Your Firm
#82	Reducing the Risks in Product Development
#85	Analyzing Your Cost in Marketing
#111	Steps In Incorporating a Business
#165	Publicize Your Company by Sharing Information
#170	The ABC's of Borrowing
#173	Innovation: How Much Is Enough?
#174	Is Your Cash Supply Adequate?
#179	Breaking the Barriers to Small Business Planning
#185	Matching the Applicant to the Job
#186	Checklist for Developing a Training Program
#191	Delegating Work and Responsibility
#193	What Is the Best Selling Price?
#194	Marketing Planning Guidelines
#195	Setting Pay for Your Management Jobs
#197	Pointers on Preparing an Employee Handbook
#201	Locating or Relocating Your Business
#202	Discover and Use Your Public Library
#206	Keep Pointed Toward Profit
#208	Problems in Managing a Family-Owned Business
#209	Preventing Employee Pilferage
#210	Records Retention: Normal and Disaster
#212	The Equipment Replacement Decision

SMALL MARKETERS AIDS (free)

#25	Are You Kidding Yourself About Your Profits?
#71	Checklist for Going Into Business
#106	Finding and Hiring the Right Employees
#107	Building Strong Relations with Your Bank
#108	Building Repeat Retail Business
#109	Stimulating Impulse Buying for Increased Sales
#111	Interior Display: A Way to Increase Sales
#112	Sales Potential and Market Shares
#114	Pleasing Your Boss, the Customer
#118	Legal Services for Small Retail and Service Firms
#119	Preventing Retail Theft
#120	Building Good Customer Relations
#121	Measuring the Results of Advertising
#124	Knowing Your Image
#126	Accounting Services for Small Service Firms
#129	Reducing Shoplifting Losses
#130	Analyze Your Records to Reduce Costs
#131	Retirement Plans for Self-Employed Owner-Managers
#132	The Federal Wage-Hour Law in Small Firms
#134	Preventing Burglary and Robbery Loss
#137	Outwitting Bad Check Passers
#138	Sweeping Profit Out the Back Door
#142	Steps in Meeting Your Tax Obligations
#144	Getting the Facts for Income Tax Reporting
#147	Sound Cash Management and Borrowing
#148	Insurance Checklist for Small Business
#149	Computers for Small Business—Service Bureau or Time Sharing?
#151	Preventing Embezzlement

FOR-SALE PUBLICATIONS (minimal cost)

Starting and Managing a Small Business of Your Own
Starting and Managing a Small Restaurant
Strengthening Small Business Management
A Handbook of Small Business Finance

Advance Preparations

Financial Recordkeeping for Small Stores
The First Two Years: Small Firm Growth and
   Survival Problems

Some other non-SBA references that may also be helpful are the *Small Business Reporter,* published by the Bank of America, *Trends in Hotel Business* by Harris, Kerr, and Forster, and *The Innkeeping Business,* published by the Canadian government. Also, the inn guides contain invaluable keys to the "little things" that make a difference.

Another source of information available to you at no charge is the Service Corps of Retired Executives (SCORE), a department of the SBA. SCORE is an organization made up of volunteers with local chapters throughout the country. Retired men and women with executive experience offer general workshops and consultation to individuals on specific matters as requested. The consultation is short-term and geared to help the business person problem-solve when struggling with a particular question. It would always be worth a telephone call to inquire if a retired executive with years of experience in your field would be available to discuss confidentially your plans and problems with you. The retired executive is a great source of expertise and knowledge whom you should not overlook when doing your preliminary study.

Another source of experience is, of course, innkeepers currently involved in the business of innkeeping. Whenever you have the chance to visit an inn and to talk with the innkeeper, ask him or her about that inn. Although innkeepers are usually very busy people, we are always pleased to discuss our work with others who are interested in the field. And you can learn a great deal just by making your own observations, too. It would be to your advantage to keep a notebook of important details to remember from your conversations and observations for use when you open your own country inn.

4

LOOKING FOR THE RIGHT PLACE FOR YOU

An intense interest in a hobby, a particular sport, a craft, or an avocation could be the springboard for helping you to decide on where you want your inn to be located—and, not so incidentally, could also provide the theme upon which your entire inn will be established. For instance, if your passion is cross-country skiing, consider opening an inn in northern New England, and organize the decor, services, and activities around the theme of cross-country skiing.

Open an inn in Gilroy, California—the "Garlic Capital of The World"—if you love to cook gourmet dishes with lots of garlic. If you are a horse lover, think about your "Old Kentucky" inn or a dude ranch in Wyoming. Open your inn near Mount Rushmore or in Vermont marble country if you are a sculptor of stone. You might open an inn along the Snake or Colorado Rivers if your passion is riding the "white water" in a raft. A desert inn makes sense for people who love the dry climate of the Southwest and the sun setting over the mesa. If you are a history buff, you could spend many happy moments welcoming like-minded guests to your inn at Concord, Massachusetts, or Gettysburg, Charlestown, San Antonio, or Eureka.

Looking for the Right Place

Our cities truly need the personal involvement that typifies country innkeeping. If you are a city person, don't hesitate to bring a bit of country hospitality to the city in the form of your "country inn." The possibilities, as you can see, are endless; that's one of the reasons why innkeeping is so exciting. The only limitations are really the limits of your own imagination and ambition.

Whatever approach you follow in making a decision on where you want your inn to be, if it turns out that you are living on one coast and you want to open an inn on the opposite cost—as was the case with us—then you have to figure out many details long-distance. Subscribing to a local newspaper will help you a great deal in learning about real estate values, properties for sale, local competition, as well as important local issues and personalities in the news. We read the weekly newspaper religiously for one year, clipping out important items—especially real estate ads and inn-related topics—and pasting them into a notebook for easy reference.

This notebook proved invaluable as time went on. It even held the name of the bramble, after which the inn was eventually named, although we did not recognize it as THE NAME when we first entered the clipping in our notebook. In one of the newspapers, there was mention of Joseph Lincoln's books about Cape Cod and his reference to a bramble tart filled with raisins that his mother used to make. Elaine also knew that there were wild and plentiful bramble roses which blossomed everywhere on Cape Cod during the summertime. Somehow, the sound of "bramble" just had a nice ring to it and Elaine wanted to remember it for future reference. Little did we know . . . !

I don't know if there are stories connected with names of other inns, but I'm intrigued by some of the "different" inn names like Barley Sheaf Farm, Redcoat's Return, The Opinicon, The Burn, Rockhouse Mountain Farm, Blueberry Hill, Inn on the Library Lawn, and the Whistling Oyster. You never know where the right name for your inn will pop up—you might find it in a newspaper, as we did.

We also read every book about Cape Cod that we could find in the Los Angeles Public Library and bookstores (not a big demand for such books in Los Angeles!). But we did find Gladys Taber and Joseph Lincoln and that was a good start on becoming acquainted with the realities and folklore of Cape Cod! When we finally did move to Cape Cod, we were already quite knowledgeable about names and places, local zoning issues, banks, other country inns, town planning committees, and many other items of interest and importance to our project. It is possible, therefore, to move into a new area to open a country inn—even across the continent—if you are willing to do some homework to make the move a success.

To assist you in finding the right place, there are more and more real estate firms that are focusing their services on the needs of country inn buyers and sellers. For instance, in Brattleboro, Vermont, there is a firm called Country Business Services, Inc., which specializes in country businesses, including inns. This firm handles about a dozen sales a year and they help people to decide if innkeeping is really for them before the sale is consummated. The would-be owner is encouraged to spend time with the innkeeper to see what the business is really like. There are other similar companies springing up throughout the country specifically geared to meet the growing interest in innkeeping and to assist people in finding just the right property.

SEARCHING FOR THE RIGHT LOCATION

Real estate brokers are partial to an old saying that there are three important factors in determining the value of a piece of real estate: (1) location, (2) location, (3) location! Whether buying an existing inn and either keeping or changing the name, renovating a building for a new use, or building a new structure—the location of the property is crucial to your inn's ultimate success.

One important reason guests will choose to stay at your country inn is its location. People will seek out and pay dearly for accommodations overlooking the ocean as is the case with the Heritage House in California; or in the heart of Napa Valley overlooking a vineyard, like the Wine Country Inn; or near recreational areas like Cuttle's Mont Tremblant Club which is adjacent to the Mont Tremblant ski area in Quebec. The Bramble Inn is located within walking distance of a lovely bay beach, and near a state park, tennis, golf, and the Cape Cod bicycle path, all of which we mention in our brochure. The Algonquin Hotel is located in downtown Manhattan—a perfect location for New York City shoppers and theatergoers. The Colonel Ebenezer Crafts Inn is located in the historic town of Sturbridge, Massachusetts, near the major attraction of Old Sturbridge Village. The "right" location can make the difference between success and failure in any business—including the business of innkeeping.

DOING A DEMOGRAPHIC STUDY

One way to determine the best location for your country inn is to do a demographic study of the area(s) in which you are interested. A demographic study will help to determine several important factors regarding the success potential of an area. One significant question to ask is how close is the nearest principal urban market from which you will attract your guests? The study will give you a picture of the overall potential of the area—its economic status, its recreational, scenic, and cultural attractions, and its current business environment. You will want to evaluate existing lodging and dining accommodations and the current need for any additional services.

Who will be your potential clientele? Will your inn be supported locally or will it be mainly a tourist-related business? If so, what are the facilities available for the traveler? Is the location easily accessible by good roads or is it so far off the beaten path that your guests may have a hard time finding you?

Accessibility to transportation is an increasingly important factor in our oil-dependent economy. Even though people seek the quaint, out-of-the-way country inn, some will need to travel by public transportation which they expect will bring them right to the inn's doorstep. Some inns are even providing shuttle service to and from airports and bus terminals for their guests' convenience.

Being located "far from the madding crowd" can be a definite attraction for those guests seeking a hideaway weekend. But there are disadvantages as well, not only in the time, effort, and *money* spent for advertising, publicity, and promotion to attract visitors to your inn, but also in the scarcity of available staff, problems in obtaining prompt deliveries and repair services, not to mention such mundane considerations as expensive toll telephone calls!

Is your prospective location zoned properly for a country inn or will you have to go through many legal hassles to do what you want to do? Are there restrictions by the town or city on future building, sign sizes, or parking? Each community has its own zoning bylaws which clearly specify what kind of business activities are allowed on any property and the number of parking spaces required for each lodging room and/or dining room. Since each municipality is different, it is essential that you find out about restrictions in your chosen community. (See "Licensing," page 68.)

Are there plans for building a super highway in a couple of years hence which will cut right in front of your sylvan hideaway? These are all questions which you should be able to answer by doing a thorough demographic study of the areas that interest you. Sources for this information are state bureaus of tourism, local chambers of commerce and town or city halls. The right location will begin to take shape more clearly for you by using this helpful tool.

NARROWING YOUR SEARCH

You've decided on one or two particular areas and now one of the biggest questions you will have to answer is whether to buy an existing inn or to create your own "from scratch." There are advantages and disadvantages to each approach, similar to the advantages and disadvantages of buying any ongoing business. Advantages include good will, name recognition, established clientele, inventory, business fixtures, equipment and supplies, loyal, trained employees, established contacts with suppliers and advertisers, and the general benefits resulting from the previous owner's labors as innkeeper. The benefits of that asset commonly known as good will should be highly valued if you are buying a successful, operating business. Although you will doubtless make changes and improvements, you are purchasing an ongoing, established business with an existing reputation which brings sales to your cash register immediately. Good will is what brings people to your inn on your first day of ownership. This, of course, is not the way with a new business which always has a period of development with start-up costs before business comes to your door. The benefits of purchasing an ongoing establishment are even greater when the previous innkeeper is hired as a consultant to the new innkeeper. I have known several instances where this has worked out to the mutual satisfaction of both parties: the new innkeeper is able to learn a great deal about his new business establishment, and the previous innkeeper is able to see the transfer of knowledge and the continuation of quality of service that had become a trademark of his inn.

The advantages of buying an existing inn dissipate quickly, however, when the business is being sold due to bankruptcy or poor profits, with antiquated equipment, rundown fixtures and furnishings, inadequate personnel, and poor credit. Those items add up to "bad will" instead of good will. When considering the purchase of such a property, you must decide if you will be buying more headaches than happiness. Purchasing such a business is not always inadvisable, but the selling price should reflect the distressed nature of the property. It could be just the right place waiting for a new owner to come in and turn the establishment into a landmark.

Related to the issue of good will is the question of the image of your new inn. If you plan drastic changes in the style and clientele of your inn, you would not want to pay a great deal of money for someone else's existing business. It probably would be wiser to start off in a new location, since it takes time to re-educate the community about your new business in a former business location. However, if there is little expense for the amount of good will involved, the location is great, and you plan major changes, then success is probably just around the corner for you.

Starting a new business in a new location gives a fresh beginning to you, your clientele, and to your community, but you have to be willing to "build the wheel" all over again. The first place you will want to visit is your city or town hall to talk with officials regarding zoning restrictions, signs, permits, parking spaces required, and so forth.

Many older properties which currently are used as country inns (and others which might lend themselves to restoration as a country inn) are located in residential areas. These existing businesses are allowed because the use often predates even the zoning bylaw. If you are contemplating running a country inn located in a residential area, it is essential to develop and maintain cordial relationships with your neighbors. They are understandably nervous that there will be noise and activity which will disturb the quiet residential quality of the neighborhood. If you operate a smooth-functioning and well-maintained inn, however, it can become the pride of the neighborhood and people will not be fearful that their property values will be diminished.

When you are evaluating a particular property, you

will want to consider the number of rooms available for lodging, the number of bathrooms available, the traffic flow throughout the building, availability of common rooms, kitchen and dining facilities, fire exits, access for deliveries, general upkeep and maintenance, room for expansion, and the extent of immediate repairs required (new roof, new septic system, wiring, and the like). In regards to bathrooms: most veteran inn-goers do not *require* private baths, knowing that old country places did not originally have a bath for each bedroom. However, the traveling American public does *enjoy* a private bath, so the more baths an inn has, the better. The availability of private baths also will allow you to charge a higher fee for accommodations at your inn.

It is also important to evaluate the space available for separate living quarters for the innkeeper and his or her family, if you are planning to live at the inn. Be sure to allocate enough living space for your needs. After a busy day of meeting the public's needs, you will require a comfortable private space of your own to rest and rejuvenate yourself.

Depending on your own needs, energy, resources available, and existing inn properties for sale, you will gradually be able to narrow your search to just the right property for you after weighing all the relative advantages and disadvantages.

Our search for the right location required 1½ years of preliminary research and nine months of actually looking at properties for sale. It required a two-week trip to Cape Cod from Los Angeles to contact some real estate agents and to decide to limit our search to the lower Cape area—from Brewster to Provincetown. Then we moved to Wellfleet, rented a house for the winter, and found employment locally. We spent every evening and weekend from September to February with real estate brokers and the "For-Sale" section of newspapers, seeking the right property to buy. We drove around the various towns and villages and became familiar with the character of the Cape and its people. We loved to drive along Route 6A — the scenic, "old Cape" road on the north side which is bordered by many large old sea captains' homes.

After looking at nearly fifty potential properties, we found the right house and location that was soon to become The Bramble Inn. We bought an old building constructed in 1861 during the Civil War which had formerly been a guest house for 25 years. The location was a very valuable one on historic, scenic Route 6A on Cape Cod. The previous business had recently closed due to the owner's death. The house had an excellent traffic flow potential among its thirteen rooms, wonderful wide pine floorboards under layers of chipped paint and linoleum, and a great deal of charm with the nooks, crannies, and pantries that old houses have. However, there were also large gaping holes in the wall plaster (hair plaster, of course), ceilings falling down, dingy faded wallpaper peeling off everywhere, and a sunroom painted aqua color over all the walls and ceiling. Outside were many lovely old plantings — shrubs, lilacs, and fruit trees. Also, there were overgrown juniper bushes in front of the house, with a well-established maple tree growing right out of them! The house had low ceilings which gave it a cozy feeling. Despite its abandoned and forlorn look, we just knew the house had "good ghosts," and that people had lived there with happy memories.

Having looked so long and so diligently, we knew we could turn this building into a successful country inn. The price was right, and the location was excellent. A builder-friend examined the house and determined that it was basically sound structurally. (You can also employ a housing inspection service to evaluate a prospective property for you from top to bottom.) The building was located in a residential zone, but since it had been used as a guest house previously, we could have a restaurant and art gallery on the first floor, and lodging rooms along with a private owners' suite on the second floor. All the place needed was a year's worth of renovation which we subcontracted, learning a great deal more about business, real estate, and people in the process! Of course, this meant that there was a full year when the cash flow was all going out; however, we were both employed during that period, and suffered no hardship.

In the property that we finally selected, we completed major renovations, redecorated throughout, created a parking lot, landscaped the outside area, changed the style of the dining room service and lodging accommodations, and gave a new name to an old business location. We were, in this way, able to take advantage of a known business site while tailoring the new inn to meet our own specifications. Six years later, however, people do still drop by to ask if this is where The Brewster 1861 House used to be. We are pleased when they do, because they say the former owner was such a nice lady and they always used to enjoy their stay so much!

If you do buy an existing business and make any changes—large or small—be prepared for criticism from the old clientele. Even though you make many improvements, there will always be those who preferred it "the old way." If you make extensive changes, you may find that the clientele for whose good will you paid so dearly may have stopped coming to your inn entirely. Hopefully, you will fill your dining and lodging rooms with your new patrons. And the lesson you will have learned well is to evaluate the comparative merits of buying an existing business or starting one of your own.

THE PERILS OF A SEASONAL BUSINESS

If the inn you open is located in an area with year-round attractions, chances are you will open a year-round business. If your inn is located in a seasonal area, however, you may decide to remain open for business only a portion of the year. Seasonal businesses are associated with some real problems of which you will want to be aware.

One problem has to do with personnel—how to find and keep good employees working with you when you are only offering seasonal employment. Transitional employees tend to be the norm for seasonal businesses with heavy reliance in the summer season on student employees. The "summer season" is beginning earlier in the spring and lasting longer into the fall in many areas lately, and students often have to return to their colleges before Labor Day, the traditional end of the summer season. Having a local population from which to draw seasonal employees helps to solve the problem somewhat, since these employees tend to be available from year to year. Some businesses offer a bonus to all employees who are able to remain through the last day of the season. Still other inns solve the problem by paying important staff members a year-round salary even though they are not working during the closed months. This helps to insure that the most significant employees will return for the next season.

Some seasonal businesses choose to extend their "high season" by remaining open during the "off season"—the slack periods just before and after the really busy months. Finding adequate staff for these periods can be very difficult. The innkeeper may find that all the transitional employees have returned to school and may be forced to do many of the daily tasks of running the inn. This may be entirely acceptable to many innkeepers, but you must be ready to do the cleaning, cooking, chambermaiding, and myriad other chores. If you are not keen on rolling up your shirtsleeves to pitch into that kind of work, then a seasonal business may not be to your liking. Maintaining a qualified, well-trained staff is a difficult problem for most businesses. When you run a seasonal inn, finding and keeping good employees is even more difficult.

Another peril for inns that are closed part of the year is the physical deterioration that can happen to the property. In colder climates, the danger of pipes freezing in a house left untended is ever present. Turning off the water and draining the pipes is the usual procedure when a building is closed for a long period. However, when a house is left unheated for a long time, wallpaper tends to loosen from the walls more rapidly. There is also the threat of vandalism to property which is left unlived in for an extended period. Some innkeepers close their seasonal businesses but continue to live in the inn as a private residence during the closed season. This alternative offers a spacious and lovely place to live in which is usually a delight to the innkeepers and their family and friends. Heating and maintaining such a large residence, however, can sometimes present a financial burden to the innkeeper.

Financial security is also an increased consideration for those who run a seasonal business. With no business income for a portion of the year, some effective budgeting is required. Cash flow may become a problem during the closed months. Adequate reserves must be set aside to cover the lean times with no income. Seasonally-run businesses experience more risk and pressure to make their money during the height of the season. What happens to inns which count on the winter ski economy when there is a winter with no snow? Imagine the pressure on seaside inns when a summer of tropical storms and rain keeps the tourists away. When your total income is dependent on just a few months of the year, it is nearly impossible to recoup the losses of a poor season. When faced with these realities, most people try to hang on and hope that the next season will be better. Undercapitalized businesses are the ones that suffer most from a poor season because they do not have the funds available to carry them over into the next season.

Having talked about the perils of seasonal businesses, we should add that there are some wonderful advantages to owning a business that runs only part of the year. You have a chance to renew yourself and your energies after working very hard and long hours during the busy season. You have time to pursue other interests and hobbies. You have the time to evaluate new directions for your business and to make plans for improvements. You have the opportunity to travel and observe other inns in operation. And all the while you are probably living in a lovely country inn that most people can only visit briefly.

5
DETERMINING WHO WILL BE YOUR CLIENTELE

Based on your demographic study, you have a good idea of the kind of population from which you will be able to draw your guests. For example, if your inn is located in the Northeast, you will be within one day's drive of the large metropolitan centers of Boston and New York. This will bring a large number of people who seek the attractions which your area offers—the seashore, the lakes and mountains, colorful fall foliage, cultural or sports events, a quiet and restful getaway, or just a homey spot convenient to a major highway where a traveler may rest and feel refreshed for another day's journey. Guests will seek you out either for your proximity to attractions in your area or for the attractions you offer directly in your inn.

WHY WILL THE PUBLIC CHOOSE TO VISIT YOUR COUNTRY INN?

An important question to ask yourself is: "Why will someone choose to stay at my inn?" Given the competition for the travel and dining dollar, what will you offer that the customer will not find elsewhere? Uniqueness is one goal to strive for—that "something special" that cannot be found elsewhere. At The Bramble Inn, the combination of art gallery with fine dining and comfortable lodging provides that uniqueness for our patrons.

In some cases, as I have mentioned before, the location itself provides that special something that draws the public. For instance, the Marathon Hotel on Grand Manan Island is directly on the route of the famous "fly over" for migrating birds; the Grey Whale Inn and the Harbor House on the Pacific Coast in California can offer the unique experience of whale-watching; and the Glen Iris Inn is just a few steps away from a spectacular waterfall on the Genesee River in New York State.

Perhaps your inn will be a large operation like the Spalding Inn Club in New Hampshire with tennis courts, golf courses, bowling greens, and swimming pool that will appeal to sports enthusiasts. Or, like the Homestead in Connecticut, you will have an elegant French restaurant that attracts the wealthy traveler. Or perhaps you will opt for a historic building that will create the ambience of a bygone era, as has been done so beautifully by the Mainstay Inn in New Jersey, the National House in Michigan, and the Old Rittenhouse Inn in Wisconsin.

There are many unique ways to give special focus to your inn which will attract guests. The Nauset House Inn in East Orleans on Cape Cod recently transported and reconstructed, pane by pane, an antique glass conservatory from Connecticut. The lovely conservatory is now an addition to their inn. Besides receiving a great deal of positive news interest, including a story in *Brides* magazine, the conservatory is quickly becoming a favorite, romantic spot for weddings. This unique construction has given a very special new focus to a previously well-established country inn.

The Outlook Lodge at the base of Pike's Peak in Colorado has chosen the perpetuation of old mountain customs as their special focus, and their guests love to

Determining Your Clientele

gather around the piano for songs from the stacks of old sheet music, and they roast marshmallows in the fireplace in this rustic setting. The red double-decker London buses at the Cheshire Inn in St. Louis, along with the Tudor half-timbered building, announce the English accent that is the trademark of this inn.

Authenticity of purpose is another reason which will attract guests to your country inn. A New England country inn with homemade quilts, period furniture, and fireplaces offers the guest an experience with traditional New England that a modern, sterile motel can never duplicate.

The innkeepers at the Lodge on the Desert in Tucson, Arizona, have taken a special care in designing and decorating the interiors of their inn to blend with the familiar Indian motifs of the Southwest, and at the Durbin Hotel in Rushville, Indiana, the decor points up the Midwest farm region in which it is situated.

Paramount in your planning is the decision as to what segment of the general public you wish to attract. This general orientation will help to determine your price structure, volume projections, and many elements of your decor, theme, and business organization. Are you seeking a select clientele that can support more expensive lodging and dining room prices? Do you plan to have a larger operation—more family-oriented—which will appeal to the middle-income traveler? Will your inn be a community-based center where town functions are apt to be held? Will there be a great deal of repeat clientele? Or will you be located in a seasonal, tourist economy where transient visitors are the rule? By deciding who you think will comprise the majority of your customers, you will begin to define these other areas as well.

Country Business Services encourages its clients to develop a written profile of their ideal guest which is based on information drawn from their demographic and economic study, as well as psychological and social characteristics. This profile then provides a solid basis for all subsequent decisions on operations and marketing.

The Inn at Princeton in Massachusetts—a truly gracious inn—has identified its clientele at the top five percent of the economic level. The food and the service are superb. Innkeepers Suzanne Reed and Elizabeth Sjogren offer more than a touch of class to their guests who have come to expect it. Guests seek out the Inn at Princeton because they know the type of establishment it is and they are willing to pay for it. The inn is geared to serving the needs of a very small percentage of the population. Because of this select market, it is essential that the innkeepers maintain a clear vision of their clientele and the services they are offering. For, should this population be lost, then the inn would have to reorganize itself from top to bottom to offer an entirely different package to an entirely different clientele. The Jamieson House in Poynette, Wisconsin, has also carefully identified its market and maintains a similarly appointed Victorian inn with special attention to preserving a turn-of-the-century elegance. The Old Rittenhouse Inn in Bayfield, Wisconsin, which must draw from as far away as Duluth, Minnesota, for its regular diners, has also established a reputation for its special ambience and excellence.

This brings us back to the basic importance of the individual innkeeper's style and personality. The innkeepers at the Inn at Princeton decorated their 19th-century Worcester industrialist's summer mansion with fine antique furniture. They are comfortable with French cuisine and elegant silver service. And after-dinner coffee in the parlor by the fire comes naturally to them. This is the ambience they choose to present to their guests.

By contrast, another innkeeper, Tony Clark, who is a rugged, outdoor sports enthusiast, chose to open a country inn called Blueberry Hill in the Green Mountains of Vermont to promote cross-country skiing. He and his wife Martha decided to serve hearty home-cooked meals and grog by the ski lodge hearth. There is a similarity of excellent service and authenticity of purpose between these two inns. They are each very different, but successful reflections of what the innkeepers' individual preferences have led them to create.

The style and personality of the innkeeper has determined which "piece of the pie" he has gone after in his business enterprise. It is essential that a new innkeeper determine at the earliest stages what kind of person he wishes to attract to his country inn. Once the market has been determined, he can go ahead with the rest of the work that leads ultimately to his welcoming that guest to sign the guest book!

TO HAVE OR NOT TO HAVE A DINING ROOM

A significant decision to make early on is whether or not to have a dining room and, if so, what kind of dining will you provide? Some inns offer a bed-and-breakfast arrangement with a continental breakfast on a buffet from which the guests serve themselves. However, let's hope you don't have any guests like the one who picked up an entire tray of muffins and whisked them off to his room. When asked later if he enjoyed the muffins, he replied, "Are there any more?"! Continental breakfasts are sometimes served on trays in the guests' rooms, as is the case with the Britt House in California. Or they can be more elaborate—full meals in themselves—and served in the inn's common area, giving the guests an opportunity to meet and socialize. Most inns find this to be the best arrangement. In fact some, like the Windsor House in Massachusetts, Blueberry Hill in Vermont, and the James House in Washington, serve breakfast in their old-fashioned kitchens.

A full dining room can be organized to serve meals only to guests of the inn, or it can be open to the general public for breakfast, lunch, and dinner, or any combination thereof.

There are several important points to be considered in the decision of whether or not to go into the restaurant business. First and foremost, do you *want* to run a restaurant? If the answer is anything less than a passionate "Yes!", it definitely would be better *not* to undertake a dining room service in your inn. Rather, make sure to locate your inn in the vicinity of several fine restaurants; enjoy providing comfortable lodgings for your guests, and happily refer them to other restaurants for their meals.

However, if your answer was a resounding "Yes!" to running a restaurant in your inn, then here are some basic points to consider. Before deciding what kind of dining service to offer, you should first evaluate the *need* for such a service. Does the area already offer many dining alternatives for your guests? Will your guests be staying several days in your inn and dependent upon you for their meals? Does your inn have the physical space for kitchen facilities, food storage, and a dining area? The size of your kitchen facilities is important, but the space does not have to be huge in order to serve a good number of people. The organization of the available space and adequate storage facilities are just as important as the actual square footage of your kitchen. Are there wholesale suppliers in the area with a constant supply available of fresh produce and high quality meats and fish?

It is essential to check with your town's or city's zoning and licensing departments, since public dining rooms have strict zoning regulations. The number of diners permitted in your restaurant is specifically limited to the square footage of your dining room, and the seating capacity determines the number of parking spaces required for your guests. These requirements are usually stated in the municipal bylaws. Whenever possible, always estimate the maximum amount of business that you might expect, so that you will be able to expand as the business grows. Some innkeeper's licenses *require* that food be served on the premises—a hold-over from the old days when inns were stops along the stagecoach routes for travelers to find food and lodging.

Once having made the decision to have meal service, you would then have to decide whether to hire a cook or to be the chef of your own restaurant. (See Chapter 7 on Running a Restaurant for further details.)

Your particular menu and manner of service will depend upon your type of inn and what you choose to present to the public. But *whatever* you serve must be of the highest quality, and *however* you serve, it must be in a friendly, courteous manner, with your guests' comfort and needs always foremost in your mind.

PERSONALITY PROFILE OF A COUNTRY INNKEEPER

If you've done all your homework, finished all your investigations, filled in your dream with all the important details, you just may be ready to become an innkeeper, and I would like to share with you my impressions of the personality profile of a successful innkeeper. As we have discussed, each innkeeper must be true to his or her own distinct personality, but there are several significant shared characteristics. First and foremost, an innkeeper enjoys meeting, working with, and being with people. He or she seeks out new situations and challenges and likes to take risks. He or she is honest and ambitious; stubborn enough to hold onto a dream in the face of adversity; flexible enough to step in wherever and whenever needed. He/she has a sense of humor and the patience of Job to deal with people's needs and whims. He/she is intelligent, well-organized, easy-going, and perfectionistic!

If this sounds like a big bill to fill—it is! However, it is impossible for even a superstar to be this way all the time.

Frequently, the personalities of a husband and wife or partners complement each other so that the strengths of each are maximized to their best advantage. At The Bramble Inn, Elaine is gregarious and a great conversationalist, so she usually acts as hostess and receptionist. Karen has strengths in personnel and business management, so she supervises the "rear of the house." Even though a division of labor does occur, most happy innkeepers have a good measure of all those characteristics mentioned in the personality profile. And, believe me, the more the better!

Success in country innkeeping is almost always a story of team cooperation; however, among the innkeepers who are "going it alone" there are some wonderful success stories. Cora Durrast has owned and kept The Tavern in Pennsylvania for more than forty years; Jane Way of the Sutter Creek Inn set the pace in country innkeeping in California; Helen Tobin at the Lincklaen House in New York State started the inn with her husband several years ago, and has been carrying on alone since his death; Gregory Burch, a young artist, uses considerable artistry in maintaining his Hawthorne Inn in Massachusetts; Bettie Gilbert ran the Colby Hill Inn in New Hampshire for years until she sold it to the Glover family. And there are a number of others: David Thomas at the Fairfield Inn in Pennsylvania; Janet Millet at the Grey Rock Inn in Maine; Patricia Corcoran at Harbor House in California; Natalie Saunders at the Pentagoet Inn in Maine; and Rush Wray at the Nu-Wray Inn in North Carolina. It's interesting that most of the above-named innkeepers are women!

PART II

Getting Your Inn Ready To Open

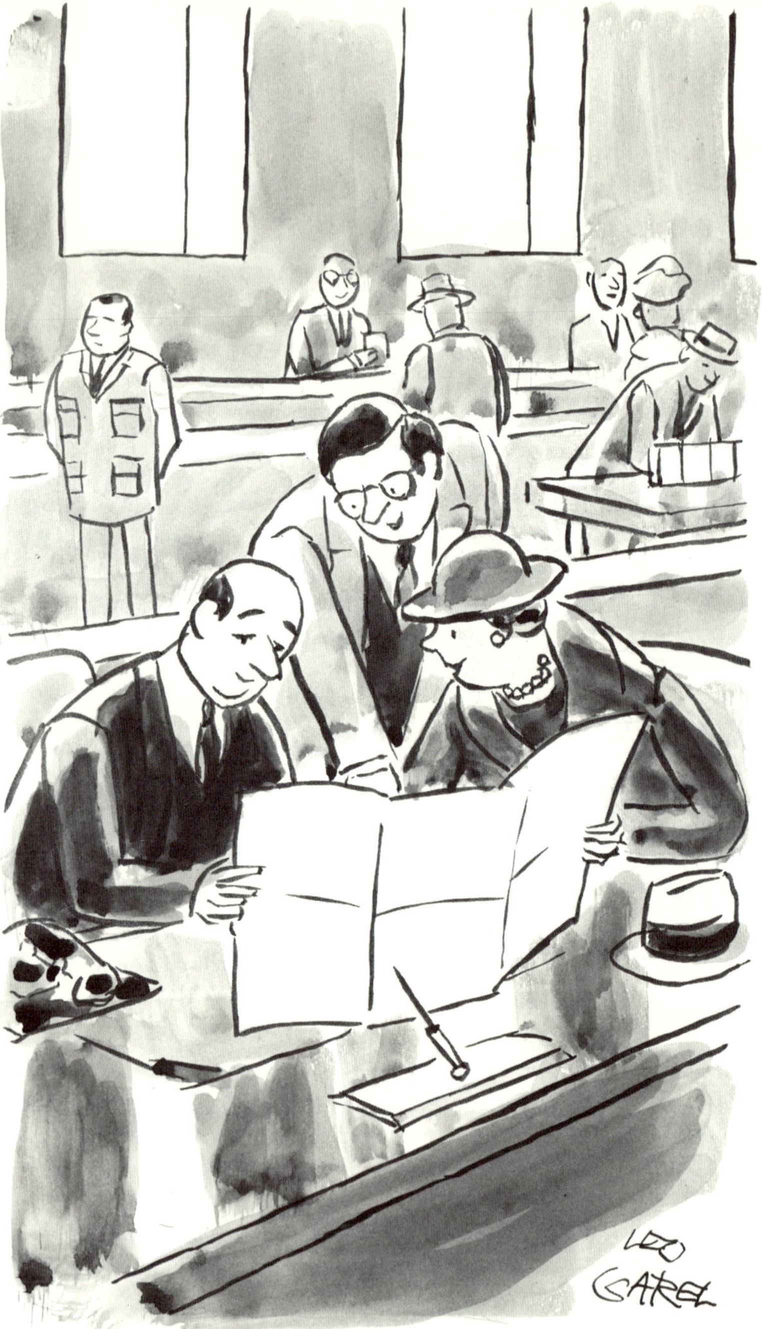
LEO
CAREL

6
THE BUSINESS SIDE OF INNKEEPING

You have finally found the inn that is right for you, the one that most fulfills your "Dream" and your "Need." Now come the excitement and the problems involved with its actual purchase and getting it ready to open.

HOW TO GET FINANCING FOR YOUR COUNTRY INN

Regardless of what economic bracket you fall into, chances are you will be seeking some sort of a mortgage or business loan when you become an innkeeper. The best time to establish a relationship with your banker when you move into a new community is *before* you need to ask for a loan! During the process of searching for the right property to purchase, we made appointments to meet with the presidents of three local banks which are active in the mortgage lending business. The year was 1974—an economic low point with a national recession in progress. Each bank president was personally gracious and supportive of our efforts to develop a new business on Cape Cod. We presented ourselves as able investors who were inquiring about distressed property which the bank might know was for sale. Although we did not learn about any specific property, we did establish the beginnings of a positive relationship with the banks—from a position of strength as investors rather than borrowers. This was very helpful when we returned several months later with a mortgage application which was positively received and approved. Bank presidents are always pleased to meet prospective clients who are anticipating opening a new business in their community. It helps them to do better business, too!

Since 1974, inflation has increased the price of real estate tremendously. Financing the purchase of all property—including a country inn—has become more expensive and more complex. In today's market, one has to consider first and second mortgages, owner financing possibilities, and complicated "creative financing" techniques. One has to rely more than ever before on the professional expertise of lawyers, real estate brokers, and bankers to unravel the complex details of financing a real estate transaction. Establishing good relationships with your bank and other professional consultants is still the best way to get the advice and support you need *before* you get to the point of arranging financing for your country inn.

Philip and Peggy Read at the Jared Coffin House on Nantucket Island told an innkeepers' meeting a number of years ago about the labyrinth they went through in order to finance the purchase of this lovely, old inn from the larger business interests on the island. The same kinds of problems occurred with the Hickory Bridge Farm in Orrtanna, Pennsylvania, and the National House in Marshall, Michigan. However, both Philbrook Farm Inn in Shelburne, New Hampshire, and Shaw's Hotel on Prince Edward Island had no such problems since they have been inns since 1860!

Ed Brummer of the Woodbound Inn has quite a tale to tell about his adventures in getting financing back in 1934. He and his partner would set out from the wilds of New Hampshire in their 1930 Ford "Beachwagon" to try to sell stock to the "wealthy people" in Boston. Armed with a load of sandwiches, which they would eat in railroad stations (which were heated), and plenty of patches for their threadbare tires which periodically blew out or went flat, they managed to round up a few interested investors—but not enough to keep afloat! Ed made a special trip to ask his 66-year-old aunt for a loan; took her to the Baldpate Inn for dinner; and then had to walk her home two miles when his "Beachwagon" broke down. And he still hadn't "popped the question!" At the end of the season, they took their records to a relative who owned and ran the Charlesgate Hotel in Boston. He went over the records and said everything looked fine, except that they hadn't done any business. Needless to say, Ed finally made a go of it—the Brummer family is still going strong with some third-generation Brummers filling in on chores around the delightful, outdoorsy Woodbound Inn.

THE USE OF PROFESSIONAL CONSULTANTS

With the purchase of your inn underway, it is important to focus as soon as possible on the realities of the business you are creating, focusing on such matters as cost-control, cash-flow, the bottom-line, and personnel administration. In order to make informed decisions, it has always proven worthwhile for us to engage the expert services of professionals—accountant, lawyer, and insurance representative.

Choosing your lawyer and accountant need not be a frustrating experience if you keep a couple of priorities uppermost in your mind. First of all, ask for recommendations from people you respect in the community: whom do they use for a lawyer or accountant? Call and ask for a preliminary appointment to meet and discuss your needs. Remember to inquire if there is a fee for this initial interview, although there usually is none. Use the intro-

GETTING YOUR INN READY TO OPEN

ductory meeting to ask specifically about fee structure and the specific charges for the service you require. It is wise to choose two or three people as potential advisers, interview all of them to compare services and fees, and then make your selection. Before you make your decision, ask yourself a few questions. Can you talk easily with this person and understand what he or she is saying to you? Are your questions being answered? Is the professional person easily accessible? Are your phone calls returned promptly? You should be able to answer yes to all these questions. After all, you are hiring this person to be a very important consultant, upon whose advice you will be making major life and business decisions. You should expect to interview such a person as thoroughly as you would a new employee.

We have an accountant who set up an easily managed bookkeeping system for us. He also prepares state and federal quarterly and year-end reports for payroll and taxes. And he prepares an annual profit and loss statement for our analysis. All other payroll and daily bookkeeping tasks, however, are done by us. We hired a lawyer to review our real estate transactions and for advice regarding the best form of business ownership for our inn. And we interviewed several insurance representatives before selecting one whom we felt had our best interests in mind. In comparing fees for services, the insurance companies showed the widest variations. For the same coverage, annual premium costs were as much as fifty percent more expensive with one firm than with another. It certainly does pay to shop around and compare value and services when selecting the support network for your new business enterprise!

FORMS OF BUSINESS OWNERSHIP

Your lawyer will make recommendations regarding the form of ownership of your new business. The three most common forms of owning a business are single proprietorship, partnership, and corporation. There are several other less widely used variations as well, such as limited partnership, real estate trust, and the subchapter S corporation. Distinct advantages and disadvantages accompany each of these forms of business ownership.

The single proprietorship is the simplest form. It offers direct owner control, receipt of all profits, and possible tax benefits to the small business owner. The single proprietor incurs unlimited liability for his business and there is a lack of continuity, should he become ill or die. A partnership can bring additional expertise or capital into the business and there is greater management flexibility with minimum outside regulation. The disadvantages are continued unlimited liability for the partners, lack of continuity, and the difficulty of finding just the right partner to go into business with.

The corporation creates a separate legal entity and thereby enjoys several advantages such as limited liability and continuous life of the business; ownership is transferable and there is only limited liability to the owners of a corporation. The disadvantages include the extra costs to establish and maintain a corporation, double taxation, and the high degree of outside regulations.

Some business people maintain that an arrangement that combines all of the benefits and few of the problems is a situation where the real estate is owned personally and then leased to a subchapter S corporation.

The Bramble Inn is owned as a partnership. But individual country inns are owned by all of the above forms of business ownership. Which one is best for you will be determined by your own particular set of circumstances.

One unusual form of ownership of a country inn is exemplified by Longfellow's Wayside Inn in Sudbury, Massachusetts. This lovely old inn is owned by the National Historic Trust which maintains the buildings and grounds for the public's enjoyment. The Historic Trust engages the innkeeper, Frank Koppeis, who welcomes delighted visitors to the Wayside Inn throughout the year.

LICENSING

Dealing with state and local licensing boards is a fact of life with which any business person must learn to contend. In general, these boards have been established to protect the safety, health and well-being of the public and the community in general. When the governing laws and regulations are interpreted by "reasonable" public servants, the goals of the business person are usually in accordance with the goals of licensing authorities. But "hair-splitting," semantics, and interpretation of the letter of the law instead of the spirit of the law can often turn your hair prematurely grey. The best advice we can give is: become as knowledgeable as you can about the laws and regulations relating to your business; try to keep lines of communications with local officials open and cordial; and believe that your self-interest is in concert with the goals of the general community's well-being.

OCCUPANCY PERMIT

If you are renovating an old structure and turning it into a country inn, the first person you will need to work with is your local building inspector. It is he who will issue you an occupancy permit after all the required renovations have been completed. The wiring inspector will come to inspect any new electrical work you have done. The plumbing inspector will check your new plumbing work. The building inspector will review any structural work that has been done. In Massachusetts, there is a state building code which mandates certain kinds of repairs to be done if over fifty percent of the house is to be renovated. This code presents great complications for the renovations of old, historic buildings because the old buildings do not conform to present-day measurements and

The Business Side of Innkeeping

materials. The goal of renovating an old building is to preserve the character of the past. But according to the code, this preservation must be done in accordance with modern health and safety requirements. It is at this point where the spirit and the letter of the law often give rise to differing interpretations.

But somehow the renovations are always completed and the occupancy permit is issued. This is a one-time permit, but the building inspector will come by on an annual basis to do inspections in order to issue your lodging house permit and your food service permit. (Each city and state may do things a little differently or call their permits by other names, but chances are similar requirements exist wherever you choose to do business.) Each of these permits costs us $25 annually. The inspector will check on items like emergency lighting, exit signs over doors, recently charged fire extinguishers, seating capacity, parking spaces, one-motion locks on doors, and general repair and maintenance.

PUBLIC HEARINGS

One type of public hearing that you may become involved in with your business usually revolves around a zoning question. The local Board of Appeals is charged with the responsibility of issuing special permits or variances which allow special circumstances for uses not currently permitted under the zoning bylaw. For instance, The Bramble Inn is located in a residentially zoned area of the town. However, the building had had a tradition of being used as a lodging house which even predated the town's zoning bylaw. Because of the "pre-existing use" of the building, we were able to purchase the property and continue its use as an inn—even though it remains in a residential zone. These public hearings are complicated legal affairs which must be appropriately advertised, abutters notified, and so forth. If there is any doubt in your mind at all about your ability to represent your interests at such a hearing, you should certainly consult a lawyer to represent you. It is usually advisable for you to be at the hearing in person to demonstrate your interest and commitment, but sometimes a legal representative can deal most effectively with the complexities of these legal hearings. Public hearings are expensive in terms of time, energy, and actual cash expenditures. When you go after a special permit or variance, you will want to do everything you can to assure a positive decision on your behalf.

ALCOHOLIC LICENSES

If you wish to serve beer, wine or alcohol in your place of business, you must obtain an alcohol pouring license. In Massachusetts, the Alcoholic Beverages Commission issues a license through the local governing body—here in Brewster, the Board of Selectmen. The process of obtaining a beer and wine license or an all-alcohol license is the same. You must petition the selectmen to hold a public hearing to review your request. All the abutters to your property must be notified at your expense by registered mail so that they can attend this hearing. You must also pay to have legal notice of the hearing advertised in a local paper. The likelihood of your obtaining a license depends on several factors: support or opposition from your abutters, the availability of such a license in your community, and competition among various businesses for available licenses. If your request for a license is granted at the hearing, you will be issued a license on an annual basis. Each community sets its own fees for alcoholic licenses. The prices usually vary according to the pressures of supply and demand. In Boston a full liquor license costs over $15,000 with an annual renewal fee of $1,600; a beer and wine license is $800 annually.

INSPECTIONS

The health inspector will visit your restaurant one or

two times each year. We had a $15 fee for the initial inspection. He or she will drop by unannounced—no doubt during your busiest day of the year—to check on food handling and storage procedures, the temperature of your refrigerators and freezers, bathroom facilities for employees, the temperature of your dishwasher water (must be at least 180°F.), general cleanliness, and safety precautions, among other things.

The fire inspector will make an annual tour of your facility, too, usually at no charge. He will point out any potential fire hazards, check your extinguishers again, the number of emergency exits, your fire escape apparatus, emergency lighting system, and make certain that the waste baskets in the bathrooms all have covers on them to snuff out oxygen from potential fires.

LOCAL REGULATIONS

In dealing with local regulations, there are always the little defeats that follow the big successes. When we received our first special permit to continue The Bramble Inn in its current location, we neglected to think ahead about the sign we would want to use. The zoning bylaw limits the size of a sign within a residential zone in Brewster to a minuscule two-foot square. There was a large existing sign which we wanted to continue to use. In order to do so, we had to go through the long and complicated Board of Appeals process once again. We were granted permission to continue to use the existing sign with the existing dimensions. This was great until we decided to hang two little signs below the big one, saying "Vacancy" and "Lunch Being Served." Since that exceeded the dimensions granted in the sign permit, we were required to remove the drop signs or pay a daily fine. So we removed the drop signs, tacked the "Vacancy" within the borders at the bottom of the original sign, and hoped the public would learn elsewhere that we were open for lunch and dinner.

From a business point of view, this was a handicap which made little logical sense to us. But from the vantage point of the members of the Board of Appeals, their responsibility is not to set a precedent that is contrary to the intent of the zoning bylaw. Being in business teaches you a sense of give and take . . . !

A *PRO FORMA* ANALYSIS

By now you have accumulated some knowledge about the fundamentals of starting your own business. You may have even selected some professional consultants to help you along the way.

The next important step is to do a "*pro forma* analysis" of your projected business. This is a "snapshot" profile of your business expectations—a projection for a specific time period showing income, costs, and a break-even point after which you will be making a profit. When you create a new enterprise with no precedents to rely on for income or cost figures, it takes a great deal of time, research, and several Kirkegaardian "leaps of faith" to put the projected figures down on paper. But you have to start somewhere; you must have a rough idea of where you want to go and how to get there. The discipline required to draw up a *pro forma* is very helpful. You will focus attention on the details which will make your inn a success and identify those areas which require rethinking in order to be profitable. (See Table 1.)

In projecting income for your lodging rooms, simply multiply the number of rooms you have to rent by how many nights you are open by the room rental rate. This will give you the maximum income from your lodging rooms at full capacity every night. You will probably want to use a lower figure in your initial *pro forma* planning for something less than 100% occupancy—perhaps 65% to 70% occupancy for your first year. (See Table 2.)

The Business Side of Innkeeping

Table 1

PRO FORMA ANALYSIS

INCOME (Estimated)

    Annual Gross Sales:
        Dining Room/Restaurant $ _____
        Lodging Rooms   _____
        Gift Shop   _____
        Other   _____

    Total Estimated Annual Gross Sales $ _____

EXPENSES (Estimated)

    Cost of Sales:
        Food $ _____
        Liquor   _____
        Giftware   _____
    Advertising   _____
    Wages   _____
    Supplies   _____
    Heat, Water, Electricity   _____
    Insurance   _____
    Interest   _____
    Legal and Professional   _____
    Equipment   _____
    Maintenance and Repair   _____
    Dues and Fees   _____
    Office and Postage   _____
    Taxes and Licenses   _____
    Travel and Auto   _____

    Total Estimated Annual Expenses $ _____

        Annual Gross Sales
        -Annual Expenses
        ―――――――――――――

        Total Estimated Gross Profit* $ _____

*Deduction of taxes and depreciation from this figure will show net profit.

Table 2

ANALYSIS OF POTENTIAL SALES— INN LODGING ROOMS

10 Lodging Rooms X $50.00 per night X 360 Nights = $180,000.00 Gross Receipts at 100% Occupancy Annually

At 10% Vacancy Rate, Gross Receipts = $162,000.00
At 30% Vacancy Rate, Gross Receipts = $126,000.00

Table 3

ANALYSIS OF POTENTIAL SALES— DINING ROOM/RESTAURANT

LUNCH 11:00-3:00	60 Seats X Turnover 2 Times X Estimated Average Check of $6.00 = $720.00 Gross Receipts per Day
DINNER 5:30-9:30	60 Seats X Turnover 2½ Times X Estimated Average Check of $10.00 = $1,500.00 Gross Receipts per Day

```
     720.00
 + 1,500.00
  $2,220.00   per Day X 6 days X 52 Weeks =
              $692,640.00 Gross Receipts Annually
              from Dining Room/Restaurant
```

The Business Side of Innkeeping

Similarly, to project your restaurant's income, multiply the total number of people you can seat in your restaurant by the number of times per meal you expect the tables to "turn over." Then multiply this figure by the average meal tab per person you expect to receive. When you multiply this figure by the number of days you are open during the year, you will have a rough idea of your gross annual income from dining. (See Table 3.) [Figuring costs and income for a restaurant operation is detailed under "Costs and Profit Margins," page 84.]

If you have other aspects in your operation, you should figure each separate department's gross income similarly; for instance, a gift shop, separate bar or lounge, separate catering or banquet functions, sports income such as golf course or horseback riding fees. For a new business, you may find that your initial projections of income were wildly optimistic or—happily—too conservative. In any case, your income projections are just half of the balance sheet in your *pro forma* analysis.

The second half, also greatly affecting final profits, is the projected costs for each department figured in the same way over the same period of time. Do your best to allocate expenses to the specific departments, although there is often overlapping between expense categories; for instance, your dining room hostess may also serve as the gift shop cashier. In such cases you can prorate a percentage of cost for each department. This shows where dollars are spent and which departments are most cost-effective.

It is helpful to obtain industry costs percentages when doing a *pro forma*. This information may be obtained from industry associations. You can compare your business costs with the experience in the general industry for expenses in personnel, advertising, food, and so forth. You can also obtain industry figures on net profits after expenses to make projections for profits for your own business. By comparing your experience with others in the same industry, you see where your good business sense is creating profits in excess of the industry's average. Conversely, you might be spending more money than you should and some economies might be introduced in certain departments.

For The Bramble Inn's seasonal business, we did a one-year, three-year, and five-year *pro forma* before ever opening our door to the public. Each year we review the previous year's actual figures and make adjustments on the five-year projections accordingly. You will find this an invaluable aid in developing both monthly and annual budgets which are an integral part of sound business practice. Along with a monthly budget, it is also important to do a deviation analysis and standard cost comparison. I cannot stress enough the importance of utilizing the *pro forma* analysis as a tool to help you to build a strong business. If you do not know where you want to go, how will you know when you get there? Once you have done the *pro forma,* keep it handy, along with your other records, for ready reference. Use this blueprint of your business to help you make decisions as you go along.

7

ON RUNNING A RESTAURANT

There have been volumes written on the subject of the restaurant business. Many people study and train for years before embarking on the ownership of a restaurant. Nearly all the factors we have covered regarding the business of a country inn apply equally to the restaurant business; location, advertising, personnel, and financing. But operating a restaurant in a country inn is like having a business within a business. Operating a restaurant is one of the most demanding jobs there is, and the failure rate of new restaurants is astronomical: ninety percent of new restaurants fail within the first five years of operation. And yet, in spite of the huge demands and unfavorable statistics, owning a restaurant is a common dream shared by millions of people. Perhaps the field is so attractive because we all know how to eat and many know how to cook. So, why not open a restaurant?

Some extremely successful restaurants are included in *Country Inns and Back Roads:* the Town Farms Inn in Middletown, Connecticut, which survived a severe fire and reopened to even greater success; the Elmwood Inn, which has the advantage of being located in a historic district in

Perryville, Kentucky; the Whistling Oyster also survived an unfortunate fire at its location on the edge of Perkins Cove in Ogunquit, Maine; the Red Inn in Provincetown, here on Cape Cod; Richardson's Canal House Inn, located on the Erie Canal in Pittsford, New York; the Welshfield Inn in Burton, Ohio; Hickory Stick Farm in Laconia, New Hampshire, which specializes in duckling; and the Farmhouse in Port Townsend, Washington, which is known far and wide as an authentic gourmet restaurant.

CAN YOU SUCCEED WHEN OTHERS FAIL?

Many of the people who tell me they are thinking about opening a country inn with a restaurant have never been in the restaurant business before. They are nervous about their lack of experience. Having presented the shocking percentage of failures among new restaurants, we are happy to say that it is possible to be successful with no formal food-service training. You will have to be doubly diligent, hard-working, creative, and lucky though, to make up for your lack of restaurant training. It may be of some comfort to you for us to describe how we opened the café at The Bramble Inn without any formal restaurant training. Again, this is not the only way to do it; but it is one way that has worked and the basic principles are sound.

Combining our talents, we had both worked several summers during our high school and college days as waitresses. In addition, Karen had managed an in-house food-service program in the social service agency she directed. We had both eaten in many excellent—and not so excellent—restaurants throughout the country, and each of us enjoyed cooking and entertaining for friends. This was the extent of our experience in the restaurant business prior to opening our own business.

We recognized our lack of formal training and experience, though, and took advantage of every opportunity to learn. We attended the New England Hotel, Motel, and Restaurant Trade Show to get exposure to food-service equipment, products, suppliers, and ideas. We were like veritable sponges as we walked up and down the long aisles at the Commonwealth Exhibition Hall, looking, absorbing, and jotting down important information and ideas on our notepads. We also continued to read everything we could find on the subject of starting a restaurant. Again, the SBA journals and pamphlets were invaluable. A lucky turn-of-events occurred which provided us with an opportunity to take a course in "Institutional Cooking" given by Walter Sinervo, longtime chef for the Cape Cod Sea Camps here in Brewster. Through this excellent course, we were exposed to "volume cooking" using commercial sized ovens, ten-gallon stock pots, walk-in freezers, two-quart measuring cups, and the like. During this course, the mystique of cooking for large numbers of people disappeared. We learned the reassuring truth that cooking for sixty people is really only cooking for six people mutiplied by ten. If you choose your menu well, have the proper equipment, and can multiply—then you can cook for large numbers of people. Actually, Brian Holmes, owner-chef at the Welshfield Inn, maintains that cooking in small quantities is the secret to good food.

WHAT TO COOK?

How do you decide what to cook? The answer to that is really very simple. Cook what you enjoy, what you know best, and what complements your environment. When The Bramble Inn was opened for its first season in 1976, our plan was to offer a limited menu which would complement the art gallery ambience. The menu included gourmet soups, Cape Cod clam chowder, fresh fruit and imported cheese plates, freshly baked bread, the Cape Cod Bramble dessert pastry, wines, and imported beers. The café and gallery were open seven days a week from

GETTING YOUR INN READY TO OPEN

10:00 A.M. to 7:00 P.M. In the morning, the café offered a "continental touch" with a light breakfast cheese plate. Since the menu was light, we planned to do a brisk lunchtime and afternoon business and an early supper trade as well.

The "limited menu" concept in restaurants was just beginning to catch on in 1976, so we were in the early stages of a new business trend. We chose this menu, however, so we could feel in control of our kitchen. Even with our minimal formal training, we could visualize exactly how these food items could be stored, prepared, and served from the kitchen, and how the various systems would work. The limited menu concept also certainly made ordering, storing and planning easier for the new restaurateurs that we had become.

A very nice thing happened! The public liked our idea! They enjoyed the art gallery and the country-elegant atmosphere we created in this old Cape Cod house. It was "different" for Cape Cod, but they liked the food and the service. By the end of the first season, our customers and our accounting books were telling us the same thing: what we had was nice, but we needed to expand the menu. People wanted a larger selection to choose from when they came to eat at the café. We could tell from the projected *pro forma* figures that the café's very limited menu of soups and cheese plates would never be financially successful.

So when we opened for the second season, we had expanded the menu and added two hot crepe entrées and a terrific quiche. We also added a second dessert item—a chocolate mint crepe (Americans prefer a chocolate dessert over anything else!). During the winter months we had experimented and perfected these recipes. We also figured out the mechanics of cooking and serving these items along with a mixed green salad with a house vinaigrette dressing. We built on our successful experience of the first year which gave us the courage to add these new entrées. And we continued to feel comfortable that our kitchen, staff, and innkeepers could manage the expanded menu effectively.

Once again, a very nice thing happened. The public loved our new offerings. The *Cape Cod Guide* even published its review of our Bramble Inn quiche as "The Best Quiche on Cape Cod." By mid-August of our second season, we could tell by our revised *pro forma* projected figures, that The Bramble Inn had "taken off" and that it had become a financial success!

Each year, we have become more able restaurateurs. We have added two more entrées to our menu in response to our customers' suggestions. The third season, we added a carbonnade de boeuf Bourguignon as a dinner entrée for the beef-eater with a hearty appetite. The fourth season we added a fillet of sole stuffed with shrimp and almonds with a Mornay sauce, since many visitors to Cape Cod request a fresh fish entrée at dinner. Over the years, we have limited our hours a bit as well. Our kitchen closes between lunch and dinner from 3:00 to 5:30 for a break. We also decided that a personally-run country inn required a day's rest—at least for the kitchen staff—so the café and gallery are closed on Sundays, although the lodging rooms continue to be open seven days a week.

Along with a limited menu, there are various alternatives to the traditional dining room service. Some inns such as the Riverside Inn in West Virginia or the Partridge Inn in Washington have specified "sittings," usually two in an evening, along with a limited menu. At the Pentagoet in Maine, a single-entrée, fixed-price dinner is served. The Graves Mountain Lodge in Virginia and the Nu-Wray Inn and Hemlock Inn in North Carolina serve their guests a family-style dinner at large, communal tables. The White Gull Inn in Wisconsin has what they call a "Fish Boil" that is held outside several evenings a week during the summer, and the fish is cooked in huge cauldrons over a roaring fire, while their guests look on in eager anticipation.

HOW MUCH TO COOK?

From would-be restaurateurs, the most anxiety-ridden question asked (even more than "what do you cook?") is, "How do you know how much to cook?" The answer is: At first you don't! At first you make the best estimate you possibly can by multiplying the number of seats in your restaurant by the "turn-over" per meal. ("Turn-over" is a convenient restaurant term indicating the number of times customers will occupy one of your seats during a given meal time.) That will give you an estimate of how many people you will be serving for a particular meal. Then you always cook a little bit extra, and hope for the best! Only with experience will you be able to anticipate the exact volume needed each day. Taking reservations is a helpful way to make estimates, but even that is not fool-proof. You will build each day's volume predictions on the previous day's experience. Eventually you will develop a sense of how much to cook, considering the fluctuations of holidays, weekends, weather conditions, and even world events which will affect the volume of your restaurant business on any given day.

Over the years, the volume of our lunch and dinner business has continued to expand. We would never have been comfortable starting out in our first year with the expanded menu we now offer. We added to the menu as we were comfortable to take on a new item. With a limited menu, we believe that everything we serve must be exceptional. We did not want to offer any item that did not meet our high standards of excellence.

HIRE A CHEF OR DO IT YOURSELF?

We are perhaps more cautious than some restaurateurs in developing new menu items because we do everything ourselves. We have chosen to be intimately involved in all aspects of innkeeping, including the kitchen. All the recipes have been personally developed by us. We then train the cook to prepare and serve the menu according to our specifications. Many innkeepers choose to handle their kitchens differently, preferring to hire a professionally trained chef to prepare his or her recipes for their restaurant. The chef may assume many of the day-to-day responsibilities of running the kitchen, ordering food supplies, supervising kitchen personnel, and so forth.

Larry Hyde of the Inn on the Library Lawn maintains "it pays to have a pro in the kitchen." He tells about the time he learned in a chance conversation that a banquet he had on his schedule for the following week was actually to take place the next night. Under the pretext of inquiring about some detail, he made a phone call to one of the sponsors, just to double-check. When that person signed off saying, "See you tomorrow night," Larry panicked at the idea of sixty people descending en masse on him and his unprepared staff. However, his chef just smiled and said, "No problem, we have enough on hand to do it." And the banquet came off without a hitch—which certainly explains Larry's enthusiasm for a professional chef.

One of the main disadvantages of having a chef is that the innkeeper is left high and dry when the chef decides to move on to other employment. And sometimes the chef may take his recipes—and your restaurant's prized reputation—along with him, if you're not careful to prevent it beforehand! The stories about chefs leaving on the morning of Thanksgiving or Mother's Day unfortunately happen all too frequently. Many an innkeeper has discovered that he or she has had to fill in on the range at the last minute when such an emergency has taken place. Many of our innkeeper acquaintances say that they are prepared to "cook the menu" at any time should it be necessary, although they do not do it ordinarily.

Whichever way you look at it, organizing your cooking staff is one of the most problematic issues you will deal with as an innkeeper. Rather than be vulnerable to the chef leaving in the middle of the summer, we decided to develop our own menu slowly and to add only items that we could perfect and master in our own kitchen.

HOW LARGE WILL YOUR RESTAURANT BE?

The number of tables and chairs in your dining room will be predetermined by the square footage required by the state building code. This seating capacity will also require a specific number of parking spaces to be available for guests. For example, in Brewster, we are required to provide one parking space for every three restaurant seats and one and a half parking places for each rental unit. It is always good to estimate more business than you initially expect; otherwise, your establishment will soon be too small.

The size of your kitchen, however, is determined by your menu preference and creativity in dealing with space. Either too little or too much space can be a problem in organizing a kitchen. The vast amount of food produced in the small quarters of a ship's galley shows that even a small, well-organized kitchen can do a big job. There are many restaurateurs who feel that time and energy is wasted in getting from one area to another in a kitchen with too much space available. Our kitchen is sixteen by thirteen feet and we feel it is a convenient size for our seating capacity of fifty people.

COST AND PROFIT MARGINS

In running a restaurant, there are two areas that eat up your potential profits most quickly—personnel expenses and food costs. With good planning and diligent supervision, you can maintain a good cost control program in both areas. Be sure not to hire too many or too few employees. Good service and positive employee morale are your measuring sticks for the optimal number of waitresses and cooks. Oftentimes, young student employees want a summer job, but they don't want to work full-time. It is better to hire two part-time workers in this case to fill one full-time position. Our cook's position is needed for sixty to seventy hours per week. We hire two people to fill this position, scheduling back-to-back dinner and lunch shifts in order to give the following 24-hours break in off-time. This seems like a good way to schedule work-time for the cook, especially in a summer resort area like Cape Cod. A general industry standard is that personnel costs should be approximately 28% of annual gross. Combined food and departmental labor costs should not exceed 65%.

Keeping food costs in line is a constant uphill battle. Before pricing the menu each year, we obtain cost figures on every food item we order from each of our distributors. Then we figure out the exact cost per serving for each menu item. This is the best way to price your menu. You will know what you must charge to make it worthwhile serving the item and you will know which are your "high profit" items. You can keep control on food costs by placing all orders yourselves. That way you can be knowledgeable about your inventory on a day-to-day basis. By ordering produce, supplies, liquor, and other food products well, you can minimize spoilage, pilfering, and wastage. You maintain a constant monitoring of what your customers are eating, what is left over, and the consistency of serving sizes. By receiving periodic deliveries you can check on the quality of the products delivered. You can also check the invoices at the point of delivery to make sure that every item has been delivered and that you have been billed properly. Do spot checks, counting and weighing, *in the presence of the supplier* so that he knows you do it. There is nothing more aggravating than beginning to make vichyssoise only to find out that the produce delivery man forgot to bring the leeks that day! Make out a delivery schedule with your suppliers that suits you and stick to it. Try to consolidate your ordering tasks as much as possible to save you time, energy, and the transportation charges often tacked on to below-minimum, "emergency" deliveries. (See also "Food Purchasing," page 106.)

On a regular basis—perhaps monthly, seasonally, and yearly—figure out your food costs as a percentage of your gross sales. The industry average places food costs between thirty and fifty percent of gross sales. If your food costs are higher, you will have to plan accordingly to offset this expense, or you will very soon be one of the satistics on new restaurant failures. When your suppliers cause your food costs to increase, you will have to find more economical ways to produce your product without sacrificing quality. Or, as most restaurateurs are forced to do, you will have to increase your menu prices. Your customers know how much food and labor costs are increasing in today's economy. They will sooner understand and accept a price increase than a reduction in quality or service. Running a restaurant is a business and you must always know what "the bottom line" is regarding costs versus sales.

Cleanliness and safety-consciousness are two other important factors in a smooth-running restaurant operation. These are values you should seek in new employees, and support and encourage them every day. We have had many people exclaim at the cleanliness of our kitchen and dining rooms—including the local health inspectors—a fact of which we are very proud. (It also makes us hesitant to eat in some restaurants, knowing how clean their kitchens are *not!*) Insisting on safe handling of kitchen equipment, immediate wipe-up of spills, availability of emergency first aid, and the like, can prevent serious accidents, lawsuits, and general inefficiency and confusion.

"FREEBIES"

A last item to be mentioned in running a restaurant is

one that most people don't talk about: What do you do about "freebies"—friends, relatives, and business associates who expect to eat and drink for free at your restaurant? Following the advice of a trusted business advisor, we decided early on that no one would be given anything as a "freebie" from the business. If we chose to bring a bottle of wine to the table to join friends after dinner, or invited relatives to stay at the inn in the off-season, then they would certainly not pay since they were our guests. However, if the same people came to dinner and were served by our waitress during regular serving hours, or stayed overnight in season, then they would be expected to pay as any other customer would. We conceptualized The Bramble Inn as a separate person who had a right to its own belongings, and to take from it was stealing. By taking from the business, we were minimizing its potential to become a viable entity.

Over the years, we have mellowed somewhat, and from time to time have relaxed this policy on special occasions. But it is helpful as a guideline in starting out—especially when every long-lost friend, relative, and acquaintance comes to see your new business. You are often faced with an awkward situation, and it is helpful to have planned in advance how to handle this situation comfortably. Remember that you can be as generous as you will with your own personal entertaining. But the business has to *earn* its existence at the end of the year when you scrutinize the *pro forma* projected figures. With every free cup of coffee, you are giving away the profits and making your business less viable.

THE RESTAURANT BUSINESS AS LIVE THEATER

Providing an enjoyable dining experience for people can be compared to creating good theater. First the stage scenes must be appropriately dramatic and well-lighted, creating an ambience which is appealing. Secondly, the timing is important, making sure that service is delivered "on-cue," not rushing or forgetting anything along the way. Thirdly, the play itself must have merit—the food must be of good quality—and must be able to withstand the critics' views. The cook is like the producer/director, the behind-the-scenes person who determines in great measure what the meal will taste like. The waitresses and waiters are the actors whose presentation, timing, personality, and delivery play such a significant role in making the difference between "eating" and "dining." (In line with this analogy, just as actors are important in "selling" a show, it is well to remember that waitresses and waiters are also salespeople who can make the difference in the amounts of checks that include such extras as first courses, wines, and desserts.) The costumes (uniforms) are important, too, giving realism to the play. At The Bramble Inn, waitresses wear long green skirts and pink or white blouses, repeating our hallmark color scheme, but also creating the feeling of a special art gallery opening every day of the season. Some inns go to even greater lengths to create atmosphere with period costumes for their staffs. For instance, Longfellow's Wayside Inn in Massachusetts dresses their waitresses in Early American costumes, while the Buxton in Ohio achieves an 1812 ambience with their staff in costumes of the period. At the Riverside Inn in West Virginia, not only the staff, but also the innkeepers themselves, dress in carefully-researched costumes of 1607. With all of these inns, there is an attention to details of architectural design, furnishings, table settings, and cuisine that set the stage for the evening's entertainment.

 The ultimate enjoyment of the audience (diners) will determine the success of the play (restaurant). It is helpful for any restaurateur to ponder this analogy to theater when he is creating a new business. Feeding people is part of the entertainment business and any successful marketing effort will have taken these factors into account.

8
ESTABLISHING THE THEME OR STYLE OF YOUR INN

Now is the time to think of bringing into being all your dreams, ideas, and plans for the theme or style of your inn, and the expression of your own identity. Being true to yourself makes fundamental business sense. By capitalizing on your own areas of interest and expertise, you can create a unique and popular inn which will attract a loyal following.

The Bramble Inn is a good example: in addition to the lodging and dining rooms, we also have an art gallery. On all the walls throughout the café, we display original works of art by local and off-Cape Cod artists. Both of us have a longstanding interest in art, and it was natural for us to establish this theme in the inn.

Elaine is a photographer who takes beautiful photos; Karen creates colorful off-loom weavings, woodcut prints, and dried flower arrangements in antique pots. The art gallery enables us not only to sell our own and other artists' creations, but also to set the theme for the entire inn. Many people interested in the arts choose to visit and stay at the inn, and the café menu is geared to the ambience of an art gallery, especially at lunch with fruit, cheese, wine, quiche, and crepes. We try each day to recreate the excitement of an art opening for each of our customers. The inn is a friendly place frequented by lovers of art, and we encourage diners to browse about the individual dining rooms to see the artwork on exhibit. The presence of the artworks creates a warm and beautiful atmosphere in which guests enjoy the experience of dining. Very often, someone will fall in love with the watercolor on the wall across the room and purchase it on the way out. When the painting is removed from the wall, there is a flurry of excitement among the diners and everyone feels that they have just participated in the promotion of art in today's world!

By capitalizing on the art gallery theme, we are able to obtain a great deal of free publicity, too. Local media are always happy to promote the new showing of an artist's work. Gallery listings are usually free as a service to the readership. It is an excellent avenue by which to keep your establishment's name before the public's eye. Our interests in art have become the integrating theme which distinguishes The Bramble from other inns.

Gery Conover at the Charlotte Inn on Martha's Vineyard has also developed an art theme with five rooms of the first floor devoted to a gallery, while Daun and Robert Martin at the Britt House in San Diego have displayed Robert's paintings throughout their handsome inn. Among the innkeepers who have transformed their entire inns into virtual showplaces of beautiful and unusual objets d'art and antiques are Jerry Ames and Chris Dickman of Red Castle Inn in Nevada, who have wonderful collections of memorabilia; Leo Bernstein of the Wayside Inn in Virginia, who has assembled what can only be described as an antique lover's paradise; and Buzz and Bobbie Harper at The Burn in Mississippi, who have created a virtual temple of grace and beauty in their lovely mansion that is filled with handsome antiques and objets d'art.

Often, the theme or style of your inn will be influenced by the location you have chosen. If your inn is by the sea, on

Establishing the Theme or Style

the desert, in the mountains, or in a place where the *location* is the *reason* for the inn, then the theme is pretty much foreordained. A desert setting cries for a ranch or hacienda with thick adobe walls to fend off the heat; a mountain fastness would seem uncomfortable with anything but a rustic, casual style; and houses by the sea need to accommodate wet feet and bathing suits and sand.

However, less overpowering locales may or may not influence your choice. Since The Bramble Inn is located in an old Cape Cod house built during the Civil War in 1861, we chose to present the lodging rooms in a quaint, country style. The old oak furniture and flowered wallpapers create a cozy and comfortable feeling.

There is probably no better example of fidelity to its setting, its historic background, nor to the personalities and style of its innkeepers, sisters Nancy Philbrook and Connie Leger, than the Philbrook Farm Inn in northern New Hampshire. In all respects—decor, furnishings, food, service, and atmosphere—this is an inn that has remained true to itself for several generations. From its woodburning cooking range to its simple, immaculate bedrooms, to its common rooms and parlors filled with memorabilia of an active involvement in New Hampshire over many years, to the sincere friendliness of its innkeepers, Philbrook Farm Inn represents a beautiful blending of authenticity of purpose and harmony with its locale.

Conversely, there is a delightful inn called the Chalet Suzanne in Florida that is a virtual kaleidoscope of around-the-world architecture from French chateau to Chinese pagoda; the Captain Whidbey has created a bit of New England on the shores of Puget Sound in Washington; the innkeepers of the Inn of the White Salmon, also in Washington, after traveling extensively in Germany have developed a Rhineland theme in their inn; and Schumacher's New Prague in Minnesota reflects the innkeepers' travels through Austria, Germany, and Czechoslovakia with eiderdown-filled comforters and an authentic Bavarian bar.

Whether or not you decide on an inn that reflects the particular locale or your own special interests depends, of course, on you. There are no hard and fast rules—only the maxim: "To thine own self be true." With that precept firmly in mind, let your imagination take flight.

REDECORATING

"Crazy" is what other people may think you are when you undertake your innkeeping endeavors. They are particularly skeptical if the property you fall in love with and purchase is in need of restoration. "Pouring good money after bad" is a saying you may hear more often than you wish. When we found The Bramble Inn, we could *see* the potential and we had a clear vision of what the place needed. Friends and family members saw more *accurately* just what *was;* they had a more realistic vision of the property, but they had no vision of its untapped potential. It isn't hard to see what is, but it takes a dreamer to see what can be.

Whenever a new owner moves into a house, the chances are pretty good that he or she won't like the previous owner's taste in decorating. Being the new owner of an inn is no exception, and redecorating is usually one of the first tasks a new innkeeper undertakes. The extent of redecorating required will depend on many factors—the innkeeper's financial resources, extent of previous upkeep and maintenance, and the theme of the new inn. Sometimes architectural changes are needed even before any redecorating is done. For instance, you may want to add more bathrooms, or make one large common room out of two smaller rooms, or build additions such as a porch, terrace, or sundeck.

If your inn is a historically significant building, you may choose to hire the consulting services of an architect or interior designer particularly skilled in the restoration and redecorating of historic buildings. Even if your inn is

Establishing the Theme or Style

not historically important, you may want to employ these consulting services to help make your inn into a beautiful showplace. Depending on your own level of skill, you may be able to do your own decorating, thereby giving your inn a personal flair characteristic only of yourself!

Before beginning to redecorate, it is important to evaluate your space needs and availability, the layout, and traffic pattern for each aspect of your business. Assign functions to different areas of the building and evaluate their effectiveness. One of the blessings of The Bramble Inn is its excellent traffic flow. It already had three stairways, three bathrooms, five exterior exits, kitchen with seven doors, four windows, and lots of cupboard and counter space. There was a pantry room off the kitchen made to order for the dishwashing and laundry areas. And there was a large rear room with a pots-and-pans double sink and space for storage, a freezer, double reach-in refrigerator, produce refrigerator, and ice-maker. The three rooms on the first floor were clearly meant to be the dining rooms as they led into one another from the front entrance and from the rear kitchen entrance.

COLOR AS A THEME

Color themes can serve the purpose of visual identification and provide a theme for your inn. When we visited the lovely Polo Lounge in the Beverly Hills Hotel in California, we were struck by the smashing color combination of pink, green, and white. Those colors later became the colors of the dining rooms at The Bramble Inn—a theme which has been carried through to the colors of the menus, tee-shirts, brochures, and stationery. We have green placemats, pink linen napkins, white tables and walls, green plants, and waitresses wearing green skirts. The combination of colors is unusual enough that many people automatically conjure up visions of The Bramble Inn when they see anything pink and green! Be sure you choose a color combination you LOVE. Anything else may lose its appeal after living and working with it daily. The color recognition may become so effective that all your birthday and Christmas gifts arrive in your chosen colors. Luckily, we still love pink and green!

In addition to a specific color scheme carried out throughout the inn, some inns achieve instant identification with their color-coordinated bedrooms, in which the curtains, bedspreads, sheets and pillowcases are in matching or harmonizing patterned fabrics—some outstanding examples of this are the Inn at Sawmill Farm in Vermont, the Homestead in Connecticut, the Charlotte Inn on Martha's Vineyard, the Lowell in Minnesota, the Waterford Inne in Maine, and the Lyme Inn in New Hampshire. Of course, the Patchwork Quilt in Indiana is noted for its displays of beautiful handmade patchwork quilts.

IMPORTANT POINTS FOR COUNTRY INNS

However you decide to manage the task of redecorating, there are certain points that all innkeepers should keep in mind: the entrance and reception area should be warm and welcoming, the common room(s) should be comfortable and inviting (a fireplace is always a treat for guests). The hallways should be attractively decorated with paintings or other wall decorations, and well-lighted with, perhaps, a lamp on a chest of drawers. (Hallways should *not* be dark, forgotten runways between each lodging room.) The lodging rooms should be nicely decorated with furniture and fabrics that suit each other. In some older buildings there are unsightly features such as visible pipes which can be hidden effectively with good decorating techniques. A country inn need not be extravagantly decorated, but some individual or unique touch should be given to each room to impart a sense of personal hospitality. Guests do expect that thought and care will have been given to the decor, however simple or luxurious it may be. Country furniture, chenille bedspreads, and rag rugs, if done well, can be as effective and inviting as elegant French wallpaper, oriental rugs, and antiques.

INCREASING ENERGY-EFFICIENCY

A final note about restoration and redecorating should include the possibilities of making your inn more energy efficient. There are many small ways that you can "retrofit" an older structure to be more energy efficient. Some improvements which can be done easily are: adding weatherstripping around doors and windows, increasing roof and wall insulation, installing storm windows and doors, and insulating hot water heaters and hot water pipes. More elaborate improvements can also be undertaken, such as installing active or passive solar systems for heating the building and/or hot water, or by simply adding a greenhouse for increased solar heating. If these efforts can be done in the early stages of redecorating, there will be money and energy savings every year to follow.

FURNISHING YOUR INN

If you have a barnful of antiques you have been collecting over the years, this could be a great way for you to furnish your country inn. Lacking a large number of family heirlooms, you can still furnish your inn with interesting pieces if you spend some time going to local auctions and flea markets or watching the "Items For Sale" listings in your local newspapers. It takes time to find just the right furniture for your inn's needs, but the process of discovery can be half of the fun. And you can still find some good "deals" if you know what you are looking for. Even the use of antique or older furnishings from mixed periods is more interesting than the plastic contemporary hotel furnishings that warehouse suppliers would have you buy.

There are some important items to include in furnishing your lodging rooms which will give your inn that homey feeling. Each lodging room should have live green plants, one or two good reading lamps, comfortable chairs, good mattresses, two pillows for each guest to lean against while reading in bed, a supply of paperbacks and other good reading material, and attractive rugs or carpeting to give the room a warm, cozy feeling. Also, don't forget to hang attractive wall decorations—paintings, photographs, or other types of wall hangings to give your rooms a more "lived-in" look.

Some inns add special de luxe touches to pamper their guests. The Captain Lord Mansion in Maine provides extra-thick, oversized towels and fluffy comforters; the Homestead in Connecticut puts clock radios and electric blankets in every room; the Bed and Breakfast Inn in San Francisco has down-filled pillows; there are Jacuzzi baths at the Inn at Stone City in Iowa; and the Inn on the Common in Vermont provides its guests with terry cloth robes for trips to a shared bathroom.

Each inn is decorated differently from the others, and that is essential to the charm of country inns. However, there are some common objectives that are shared by every good country inn: cleanliness, harmonious surroundings, good taste, comfort, and gentility. Beyond these, each inn decorates according to the innkeeper's personal preference and the style of the inn. You will, however, see a good number of oriental rugs, old pine hutches, chenille bedspreads, and Early American primitive paintings as you make the rounds, visiting country inns!

9
PURCHASING FOR YOUR INN

EQUIPMENT AND SUPPLIES

Being a smart shopper does not always mean buying the least expensive product. It does mean comparing quality and prices and buying the best product available to suit your needs in your price range. In purchasing equipment and supplies for a business, the best way to know what is on the market is to visit wholesale supply houses which sell to members of the trade. In any large city there are many such wholesale supply houses. They carry a wide variety of restaurant, motel, and hotel supplies and equipment from glassware to towels to meat grinders. We have found that there are substantial price differences even among wholesale suppliers. Usually the businesses with the most attractive display showrooms and the largest outside sales force charge the highest prices. By comparison-shopping and talking with other consumers in the business, we were able to locate a supplier with a warehouse off the beaten path in Chelsea who consistently offered us the best prices anywhere. He is small enough to give us personal service and large enough to get us anything we need. His prices usually fall between ten and twenty percent above his cost, plus delivery charges. The first time we visited his showroom, however, we were aghast with the apparent disarray. Having been accustomed to department store shopping, we were amazed to see the products displayed so haphazardly among the clutter and dust of a warehouse. We have now become used to supply-house shopping and know that it makes financial sense to buy the product at the best price— not necessarily displayed in the prettiest manner. Merchandise displays cost *you* money—even in a wholesale supply store.

SAVE MONEY—PAY PROMPTLY

Another cost-saving tip in purchasing is always to review the terms of payment which usually appear at the top of the invoice. There is often a discount given for prompt payment. For example, "2-net 30" means that 2% can be deducted from the total invoice if payment is made within 30 days. Similarly, "5-net 10" means 5% discount can be deducted if the bill is paid within 10 days. If you plan to pay with cash, always ask your supplier if there is a cash discount. Because he works on tight cash flow and many customers buy on credit, he may offer a 2% discount for immediate payment—depending on his margin of profit on the sale of the particular product.

IMPORTANCE OF GOOD SERVICE PEOPLE

No price break or discount is worth the sacrifice of good services. As Murphy's Law predicts, your oven *will* break down on a busy holiday weekend. Your dishwasher door *will* jam and refuse to close tight during another busy dinner. Your hot water heater *will* spring a leak and need to be replaced on the Fourth of July! We know because all of these things have happened to us! Having a dependable supplier—one who will work with you to help you over the trouble spots—is worth its weight in gold—literally!

If your service man is also a supplier it is well to buy from him. Always keep your service instructions and telephone numbers, warranties and model numbers nearby and readily available, too, so you will know if a repair or replacement is covered by the warranty.

It might be worth mentioning here for many inns whose water supply is a well on the property, keeping the electrician's and plumber's telephone numbers handy is a must. The stories about country inns whose water supply failed on Christmas Eve or at the start of the Fourth of July weekend are too numerous to ignore.

BASIC SHOPPING LIST

To give you an idea of the wide variety of equipment and supplies we researched and purchased before opening our inn, I have set aside some space below. This will give you a checklist, too, to consider what you need to purchase. Since neither of us had formal training in purchasing for an inn, we used our common sense and experience in shopping for home use multiplied by the need for greater volume and durability. Because we did not want to be too "institutional," we often rejected an item which was traditionally used by a restaurant and spent more time and energy seeking the unusual—such as open salt and pepper cellars with individual glass spoons in place of ordinary shakers. It is this kind of purchasing effort which has given the distinctiveness to The Bramble Inn which people seem to appreciate and delight in.

Here is the shopping list we wish someone had drawn up for us. We hope it will help you along the way of opening your country inn! It is a basic list, but not all-inclusive.

SHOPPING LIST FOR A COUNTRY INN

RECEPTION AREA

- Desk or counter
- Key cabinet or holder
- Cash register
- Rug
- Lamps
- Plants
- Pictures
- Wastebasket

COMMON OR PUBLIC ROOMS

Furniture
- Sofas or settees
- Armchairs
- End tables
- Occasional tables
- Coffee table
- Reading lamps
- Bookcases
- Cabinets or shelves for game storage
- Writing desks
- Curtains or draperies
- Rugs

Accessories
- Plants
- Decorative pillows
- Pictures or other wall decoration
- Fireplace equipment
- Decorative items for tables and shelves
- Magazines/books
- Television
- Stereo system or hi-fi
- Fans and/or air conditioners
- Ashtrays
- Games

Purchasing for Your Inn

　　　　Wastebasket

　　Required equipment
　　　　Fire extinguishers
　　　　Smoke detectors
　　　　Emergency lighting system

DINING ROOMS
　　Furniture
　　　　Tables
　　　　Chairs
　　　　Sideboards or cabinets
　　　　Serving stands
　　　　Curtains
　　　　Rugs

　　Table linen
　　　　Placemats
　　　　Tablecloths
　　　　Napkins

　　Flatware
　　　　Knives (dinner, steak, bread-and-butter)
　　　　Forks (dinner, salad, relish)
　　　　Spoons (tea, soup, iced tea, sugar)

　　Dishes
　　　　Plates (dinner, salad, bread-and-butter, dessert)
　　　　Soup bowls
　　　　Sauce or vegetable dishes
　　　　Cups and saucers or mugs
　　　　Underliners

　　Glassware
　　　　Water pitchers
　　　　Water glasses
　　　　Wine goblets (red wine, white wine, sherry)
　　　　Iced tea glasses
　　　　Pilsner glasses
　　　　Bar glasses

GETTING YOUR INN READY TO OPEN

Accessories
- Coffee service
- Sugars and creamers
- Salt and pepper cellars
- Butter dishes
- Relish trays
- Bread baskets
- Table vases
- Dried flowers for vases
- Candleholders and candles
- Ashtrays
- Napkin holders
- Plants
- Wall decorations

Now you have your table set! Moving into the kitchen, your shopping list continues:

KITCHEN

Built-ins
- Sinks (including pots-and-pans sink)
- Work/serving counters
- Cupboards and shelves (dishes, pots and pans, equipment)
- Drawers (flatware, utensils, towels and uniforms)

Large appliances
- Stoves and ovens
- Refrigerators
- Freezers
- Ice maker
- Commercial dishwasher
- Commercial hot water heater

Small appliances
- Food processor
- Commercial blender

Purchasing for Your Inn

    Mixer
    Slicer
    Toaster
    Coffee maker
    Food scale
    Can opener
    Fans and/or air conditioners

Equipment
    Cutting boards
    Mixing bowls
    Saucepans and lids
    Stockpots
    Skillets
    Pans (roasting, baking)
    Covered storage containers
    Refrigerator dishes
    Casserole servers
    Crepe makers
    Measuring cups (1-2 qt.)
    Strainers
    Measuring spoons
    Wooden spoons
    Stirring and slotted spoons
    Chef's knives
    Long-handled forks
    Ladles
    Spatulas
    Cleaning and paper supplies
    Waste bins

And now the shopping list for your guests' bedrooms and baths:

BEDROOMS (Doors with locks and keys)

    Furniture
        Beds
        Box springs and mattresses

GETTING YOUR INN READY TO OPEN

    Armchairs or straight chairs
    Tables or writing desks
    Dressers or chests of drawers
    Reading lamps
    Curtains
    Mirrors
    Luggage racks
    Rugs

Linen
    Mattress covers
    Sheets
    Blankets
    Pillows
    Pillow cases
    Bedspreads
    Runners or scarves for dressers or bureaus

Accessories
    Fans and/or air conditioners
    Ice buckets
    Glassware
    Coat hangers
    Plants
    Books/magazines
    Writing materials
    Pictures or other wall decorations
    Waste baskets

BATHROOMS

    Wall cabinets or shelves
    Mirrors
    Shower curtains
    Bath mats
    Rugs
    Bath towels
    Hand towels
    Face cloths

Purchasing for Your Inn

    Drinking glasses
    Soaps
    Bathroom tissue
    Waste baskets

OTHER POSSIBLE GATHERING PLACES

    Porches
    Game room
    Music room
    Lawn area
    Swimming pool

(Each of the above areas requires its own special equipment and furnishings.)

And here is the shopping list to help keep your inn clean and sparkling:

LAUNDRY ROOM AND CLEANING AREA

    Built-ins
        Counters
        Storage shelves
        Closets
        Tubs or sinks

    Appliances
        Clothes washer and dryer
        Vacuum cleaner
        Iron

    Furniture
        Tables
        Chairs
        Ironing board

    Miscellaneous
        Laundry bins
        Trash barrels

Pails
Mops
Brooms
Brushes
Sponges
Laundry & cleaning supplies
Paper goods

FOOD PURCHASING

The purchase of major equipment and furnishings is usually done once with periodic replacement for breakage and updating equipment. If you serve food, purchasing becomes a more time-consuming task and a daily concern. Ordering well can make the difference between a profit-making operation and a failure. The kitchen manager must have excellent control over purchasing, allowing for little waste and spoilage. Without careful purchasing, many profits are thrown out with the garbage or washed down the drain.

If quality and dependability are equally available, it is wise to do business with one major food service supplier. This saves you time in placing orders, receiving deliveries, and writing checks for payment. However, if you can only get the quality product you are seeking from a different supplier, it is worth the extra effort. We purchase our basic staples and most of our non-consumable supplies from a large national food service distributor with delivery once a week as needed. We buy our produce from a second local wholesale supplier who delivers daily. We purchase our meat and fish from local retail stores where we personally do the marketing in order to obtain the best product available. Our milk and dairy products are delivered three times a week by yet another supplier. And a local baker delivers freshly baked bread each morning. You can readily see how the coordinator of purchasing plays a vital role in the success of the kitchen. With six separate suppliers to work with—most on a daily basis—the getting of supplies consumes a large amount of time, energy, and money. In operating The Bramble Inn, we chose to do these tasks in order to have close control over the expenditures and an intimate knowledge of the inventory.

WINE AND BEER PURCHASING

If you choose to serve beer and wine or alcoholic beverages, you will be required to obtain a liquor license from the local licensing body. Availability and fees for these pouring licenses vary greatly, depending on the demand and competition among local businesses. In the state of Massachusetts, a full liquor license, when available, costs between $15,000 to $20,000 in Boston with an annual renewal fee of $1,600. A beer and wine license is easily available at $800 a year in Boston and even less in smaller cities and towns.

The selection of fine wines requires years of study and experience. Even for a knowledgeable person, it is usually necessary to rely on the recommendations of the wine salespeople from wholesale distributors. They will visit your country inn for orders and keep you abreast of new wines which are continually coming on the market. Your wine salesperson will also be able to project the continued availability of certain wines before you decide to include them on your wine list. Tradition has it that a host is judged by the house wine he pours. It is important that you choose an excellent house wine that will reflect the good taste of your establishment. Unfortunately, in the United States this tradition has not been adhered to and house wine often becomes the cheapest low-quality wine offered by the house.

Because of the multi-layered and often confusing system of liquor and wine distribution, you will no doubt have to deal with a large number of suppliers, depending on the extent of your liquor service. Because each supplier has a minimum order requirement, usually $100, it is helpful initially to consolidate your ordering as much as possible. You can always expand as your public demands new items for consumption.

PURCHASING TIPS

Here are some additional hints for successful purchasing: keep copies of all your invoices and delivery slips and file them for easy accessibility. Pay your bills when they are due; never be caught paying interest charges for late payment—it just doesn't make sense! And take advantage of discounts for early payment when offered. Everyone has a "cash-flow" problem from time to time, but the efficient business person plans ahead for those times and never runs the risk of developing bad credit with his suppliers. Don't be afraid to do some comparison shopping with your suppliers' competition. You will be able to judge for yourself if you are still getting the most for your money. Don't be quick to abandon a long-term positive relationship with a dependable supplier, however, just because a new one offers an attractive bonus or sale item. Sometimes it is worth a few more pennies per pound in order to have top quality products, delivery, and service. Only you can make that judgment for yourself.

10
PERSONNEL

Let's review where you are and how far you have progressed in becoming an innkeeper. You have decided on the kind of inn you want to run and have found the right piece of property. You have chosen the form of business ownership which best suits your circumstances. You have developed a theme and focus which is reflected in the remodeling and decorating of your inn. You have purchased your equipment and supplies, and have lined up wholesale distributors for your foods and liquors.

After you have laid all of the above groundwork, your next task is to attract capable, service-oriented, dependable and loyal employees. And, once you have trained them, the goal is to keep them with you. A veteran businessman once told us that the most difficult part of being a personnel manager was dealing with people! We strive to create a feeling of "family" among staff members. And this close feeling allows for the spirit of innkeeping that the guests cherish so much. Especially in a small country inn, it is important that employees are cooperative and able to work well together.

ORGANIZATION OF PERSONNEL

The following describes the personnel structure and organization for The Bramble Inn. Each inn is different and will have its own distinct personnel needs. But this is how The Bramble Inn works: for our summer season, we hire five or six waitresses, two cooks, two chambermaids, and two dishwashers.

If you have a large inn, chances are you will employ the services of a janitorial service and a rubbish collector on a daily basis, in addition to chambermaids for the lodging rooms. For care of the landscaping, you will probably hire a grounds crew to maintain the outside of your property—mowing lawns, pruning, fertilizing, planting, watering, and the like. If you have a small country inn, all of these same tasks still have to be done, if only on a smaller basis. You will need to have some help with these regular tasks, because it is impossible to do everything yourself.

The smaller the inn, the more direct supervisory work you will do with employees. We personally train new employees. Because we can and have done each job assigned to an employee, it is easy to demonstrate our expectations. For each job, there should be a clearly defined set of duties and responsibilities. A written job description for each position may be a helpful tool to develop. If the employer neglects to give adequate direction, he cannot be upset when a new employee doesn't do the job right.

Whenever possible, we prefer to hire local residents as employees. There are several benefits to this policy. The likelihood is greater that a trained employee will return for the next season, and the salary remains in the community and benefits the local economy. Relationships between the business and residential communities are enhanced through local employees. We also offer advancement possibilities to the present staff whenever we can. In larger businesses with more employees—perhaps including positions such as receptionist, bus people, maitre d', sous chef, and cashier—

there is even more opportunity for advancement and training within the organization.

It is important to pay your employees as well as you can. A well-paid, loyal employee is a walking advertisement for your business and will bring you many benefits. If you are able to pay even a modest amount above the going rate for a valued employee, you will find it worthwhile. The federal government does not require businesses grossing less than $325,000 per year to pay employees the minimum wage ($3.35 per hour as of January 1, 1981). However, by paying at least the minimum wage to even entry-level employees, you can reward the responsibility and hard work you expect from your help. It is essential to pay your employees promptly, since you expect promptness from them each day of work. We have also found that posting the work schedule promptly on a weekly basis gives employees the chance to plan ahead and know what you will be expecting from them. Extremely well-organized staff procedures have been worked out carefully by Ken and Wendy Gibson for the very busy restaurant in their Robert Morris Inn in Maryland. Each new employee is thoroughly trained, and they, too, post work schedules in the kitchen. In general, the better organized you are, the better organized your staff will be. They will learn from your example. If your style is "last minute," you will probably find many crises cropping up for your employees at the last minute, too!

To promote the "family feeling" mentioned earlier, we instituted a traditional annual staff party at the end of every season. This is an excellent time to summarize the growth and progress of the business, and to publicly recognize the contributions of each and every employee—from estimating the number of dishes the dishwasher washed during the season, to how many beds the chambermaid made, to how many quiches the cook cooked! The party is a way of engendering good feelings among staff members and encouraging employees to return for the next season. Everyone finishes the summer season with a good taste in his mouth—literally—since we traditionally serve a hearty and delicious chili!

THE OMNIPRESENT INNKEEPER

In a small country inn such as ours, it is quite common for the innkeeper to pitch in and perform any task that needs to be done. When the cook is ill or the dishwasher has to attend the senior prom, guess whose help is often called upon? The innkeeper of a small country inn can—and at times does—wash dishes, wait on tables, make beds, and cook! And every innkeeper knows he must be ready to do these tasks whenever necessary. All of which reminds me of the story Ed Brummer tells of his early days at the Woodbound Inn when his partner did the laundry, and evidently was terribly slow about it. Ed would have to shout down the cellar stairs for him to hurry up with the napkins as they were needed for the guests who were already sitting down in the dining room!

On a regular basis at The Bramble Inn, Elaine acts as a hostess, cashier, and receptionist for the inn's café, gallery, and lodging rooms—covering the "front of the house." Karen is responsible for the "back of the house"—supervising the kitchen and dining room staff, placing orders, receiving deliveries, and checking that the food is prepared and served to our standards. Elaine supervises the chambermaids and dishwashers, each one having a separate assignment. There are no bus boys or girls since the waitresses and waiters clear and reset their own tables. But on busy rainy days Elaine and Karen do clear tables when necessary so that our customers can be served more quickly.

This personnel structure will not work for every inn since the needs of each business are different. When you are at this point in developing your inn, visit other inns and ask whom the innkeeper employs to fill which positions. Observe how the inn is run and by whom. Then decide how you want to run *your* inn. Which functions do you want to perform and which ones do you want to delegate to someone else? The larger your business, the more you must delegate in order to free your time for management decisions.

If your inn is a small and intimate one, you may have chosen it *because* it allows (read: "requires") you to be involved in the day-to-day operation of the business. In a personally-run country inn, the public soon comes to expect that you will always be there to welcome them no matter when they come to stay or dine. This, ideally, is a lovely fantasy wherein you are always available to welcome your guests. In reality, such an expectation is unreasonable for either you or your public to have; you would soon become a prisoner to your inn with eventual negative results. It is important that your "presence" be available at all times at your inn. However, you can be away for a time if your have delegated responsibilities to a well-trained and gracious employee. Many innkeepers have learned that it is wise to plan at least two to three consecutive days a month for their own "free time" away from the inn. Admittedly it takes quite a few years and a well-trained staff to accomplish this, but the Captain Lord Mansion and Goose Cove Lodge in Maine are two examples of inns where innkeepers conscientiously try to get away from the inn and spend some time for themselves.

Being an innkeeper of a small, personal country inn does make great demands on your time and availability. If you know about these demands ahead of time, you can decide what kind of innkeeping you want to become involved in.

11

GETTING YOUR STORY TOLD

There are a variety of ways to let the world know who you are and what you have to offer. The necessity for making your presence known cannot be too heavily stressed, especially if you are off the beaten path. Advertising, which requires immediate cash and can be very expensive, has an important place in your plans. Although it is difficult to measure the direct ratio of advertising dollars to sales, the fact remains that unless you put your name before the public, the public will remain unaware of your existence. Pinpointing your potential market is probably the single most important and most difficult component in planning an advertising campaign and should be investigated thoroughly. Basically, getting your brochure into the hands of as many people as possible is one of your best advertising approaches, and the distribution of it should be one of your main advertising objectives.

Publicity can be extremely effective and has the added attraction of usually costing little beyond some planning, time, and energy. Promotional projects are wonderful devices for obtaining attention for your inn. You will need to employ all of these methods at one time or another as aids in arousing the interest of the public in your inn and, hopefully, inducing it to pay you a visit. In evaluating the comparative effectiveness of any one approach, it behooves you to try to determine how your guests learned about your inn.

ADVERTISING

Your advertising budget can quickly swell to unbelievable size if limits are not set early. Think of each year's expenditures as an "advertising campaign," a specific effort with a specified budgeted dollar amount to attract customers. At the end of the year, you can evaluate how well your "campaign" did. Set yourself a plan and a goal to try new sources of advertising over a period of time to determine which ones are best for you. Remember, however, to give any one place a long enough trial period since continuity is an important factor in the success of an advertising program.

In establishing The Bramble Inn, we knew the personal, quaint, individualized image we wanted to create. We chose not to work directly with an advertising agency because we did not want that "plastic, polished look" that we were afraid an agency would want to mold us into. In hindsight, we initially might have benefited from exploring more fully what an ad agency could have done for us. As it happened, we waited until our third year in business to develop a logo, and to have stationery printed! This certainly is the area which showed our cautious optimism most clearly, thinking only of the reams of business letterheads which would be wasted should the business fail! It was a happy day when the business stationery with logo—and even tee-shirts with logo—appeared, heralding our feelings of stability and success at last!

When we first opened our inn, Karen's greatest fear was that no one would come and that the business would flop. Elaine's greatest fear was that everyone would come and we would be overwhelmed. Because we knew that The Bramble Inn would appeal to people eventually through "word of mouth" advertising—and because of Elaine's fear that we would be deluged with throngs of people—we did very little advertising or promotion for opening day. That proved to be a mistake and our business initially got off to a slow start. All the manuals warn new restaurants against promoting a big opening-day celebration. They caution you to break in slowly your new equipment, systems, and personnel and make certain that you can handle the business that comes to your door. They advise it is better to start off slowly than to alienate potential customers by serving them poorly because you are too busy on opening day. The best alternative seems to be to open quietly for a few days to get the "kinks" worked out of the operation. Then hold an opening-day celebration soon after everyone is trained and ready to handle the crowds. Word-of-mouth advertising is the very best way to expand your clientele. But it is a very slow way, showing results usually only after years of painstaking service. Don't pass up some good opportunities for promoting your business from its very first opening day!

PINPOINTING YOUR MARKET

In determining where your market is, you must first decide what is the nature of the services your inn provides. For instance, if you have a restaurant which caters to the public, then your most immediate market will be local, perhaps extending to a thirty or forty-mile radius. The market for your lodging rooms will, of course, extend much farther, and the nearest major city becomes your principal target.

For your restaurant operation, an advertising campaign should be mapped out for as many local newspapers as possible, using a series of ads on a rotation basis. Remember, the same people are going to be seeing your ad every week, therefore make them interesting and eye-catching.

Frequent small-space ads in the travel section of the nearest major city's newspaper or in a regional magazine will attract attention to your lodging rooms. During the off-season, many of the inns have special midweek rates or packages that include dinners, overnight lodgings, breakfast, and sometimes admission tickets to various local entertainments, all included in a single price. During the times when you are not advertising some special offering, it is well to remember you are going to sustain the readers' growing awareness by running a series of smaller ads. Look upon such advertising as an investment and try to avoid thinking that "we'll just try it and see what happens." Always choose publications that are well-printed and produced.

When you feel comfortable about spending additional money, find suitable media in another major market and repeat this same process; but remember, the results from the more distant market will not be the same as those from a nearer, more logical weekend market.

There are a number of inns that use small-space advertising most effectively; among these are several in Pennsylvania: the 1740 House, the Pump House Inn, and the Inn at Starlight Lake; also, the Whitehall Inn and the Captain Lord Mansion in Maine, the Beaumont Inn in Kentucky, the Bird and Bottle in New York State, and the Inn on the Common in Vermont. You may have seen some of their ads in the *New Yorker*. Most inns concentrate in their primary market area, depending upon the importance of the dining room in their plan, and others advertise in the classified sections of such publications as *Early American Life, Yankee,* the *Smithsonian, Americana,* and the *Christian Science Monitor.* Using such national magazines can be very helpful; however, in all cases, it is necessary to encourage the reader to send for your free brochure and to key the ads in such a way that you will know which publication is providing you with the most responses. A high response at this level does not necessarily mean an influx of new guests, so it is necessary to try to trace down, if possible, where your guests learned about your inn.

DEVELOPING YOUR BROCHURE

As mentioned earlier, your brochure is your most important advertising tool and should be planned with extra-special care and thought. In developing a brochure for The Bramble Inn, our goal was to incorporate all the elements that we wanted to use to characterize our establishment. These included the use of green parchment paper, hand-lettering, and a sketch of the actual inn. The sketch has become our logo which enlarges and reduces well. More important, it tells people what the inn looks like and promotes the feeling of warm hospitality engendered by "hearth and home."

Developing a brochure is a service which can be purchased from an advertising agency. However, we characteristically felt that with some research we should be able to do it as well and less expensively on our own. The first step was to collect and review as many copies of brochures as we could obtain from other inns, hotels, and the Chamber of Commerce. Again, we decided what elements we liked best from a variety of formats and went ahead writing our own copy, doing our own layout, and bringing it all to the printer. The hardest task we had was finding a printer with the right shade of green paper! Such a colored paper is an unusual request—good for the purpose of visual recognition but a problem for getting brochures printed. After a good deal of searching, we finally had to purchase a full case of "Bramble Inn Green" paper—of which we use a portion each year for new brochures and menus. At the very least, we don't look like everyone else! And that is the biggest drawback to working with an advertising agency. There seems to be developing a new style which might well be called "country inn chic."

The innkeepers of two gracious and lovely country inns were recently sharing brochures. The similarities of the brochures were unmistakable—from the layout, to the print style, and even the border design. They were obviously created by the same agency to achieve that "quaint, country inn look," which may lose its uniqueness if many more country inn brochures are designed by this agency!

DEVELOPING AN EFFECTIVE DISPLAY AD

If you have a limited advertising budget (who doesn't?), you might place a large initial ad to "tell your story." Then use "reminder ads" which are small ads with your name, address, and limited copy—just enough to keep your name in front of the public. Sometimes large newspapers have left-over space for single-line ads. They sell these one-line ads for a minimal cost even for front page coverage. Placement of ads on a page is important for their effectiveness, too. The best place for an ad is on the outside, right-hand column on a printed page. Remember to request this placement for your ad—even though it cannot always be assured.

In creating an ad, it is tempting to try to say too much in too small a space. "White space" in an ad is often as valuable as the printed copy in capturing attention, after you have said your basic message. To develop an effective ad, first spend some time looking through newspapers and magazines for ads that catch your eye. Clip the ads out and review them to evaluate what made your eye focus on them. When you identify those eye-catching qualities, use them in your own ads. You, too, should have successful ads which bring in customers.

Most newspapers offer the services of their art department at minimal or no charge to develop an attractive ad and to encourage your advertising with them. With written advertising copy to be used for newspaper or magazine ads, we chose to use hand-lettering to create a distinctive, personal look. We continued the hand-lettered theme in our inn brochures, postcards, and menus, as well as in other promotional material.

VISUAL IDENTIFICATION

If you did not want anyone to know where you are or what you are doing, you certainly would not be doing any advertising. You choose to spend your hard-earned money on ads in order to have your country inn identified and visited by new customers who want to purchase your services. The goal of achieving visual recognition should provide a basis for your decisions in advertising.

Consistency enhances identification. If you use the same border around all your ads or the same copy itself in several different newspapers, the image is reinforced each time the reader sees the ad. When an ad agency or art service helps to develop a logo for your country inn, the sign is such that it can be enlarged or reduced. It is easily identified and legible in all sizes. You want people to look at your logo and immediately think of you.

Our choice of pink and green as the color theme for our inn also provided us with a tailor-made visual identification. By repeating those colors, not only throughout our inn, but also in our menus, brochures, and stationery, we have established instant recognition through color for our inn.

RADIO ADVERTISING

One of the most expensive forms of advertising which is also very difficult to measure for a direct response to dollars spent is radio advertising. We have used this only sparingly to announce our reopening each season. To be most effective, radio ads must blanket the airwaves with your message. Listeners must hear your name several times a day, several times a week before they will remember it. But radio advertising has several distinct benefits that often make it a good buy for your advertising dollar. Radio tends to reach a different audience than the printed word does. It is often a "captive audience," perhaps driving to work or doing the breakfast dishes. It reaches a passive audience who does not even have to turn a page to discover you. By choosing a particular station format (FM or AM, "Top-40," Classical, Light Rock, Easy Listening), you can send your message to the audience of your choice. It is essential to analyze your potential market before selecting a radio station for your ads. It is also helpful to listen to your guests' comments about how they learned of your inn—in order to evaluate the effectiveness of your entire advertising campaign.

The radio can be an excellent advertising tool, but you must be watchful that your advertising budget does not just evaporate on the airwaves. Seek all the advice you can from the station for composing the copy, selecting background music, and the right voice to present the image you want to convey to the listening audience. You want to create a message that, in a very brief time, will make people stop, listen, take note of you, and follow up with a visit to purchase your product. You might even want to consider recording your ads yourself since the "personal touch" and a unique voice on the radio often packs a powerful punch.

One of the most successful radio campaigns which used a nearby primary market and emphasized lunches and dinners, was actually written and taped by a former innkeeper who was himself a very interesting personality connected with the inn. These were not the bland "canned" announcements that are sometimes prepared by radio stations, but had a touch of wry humor and it was easy to trace their effectiveness because a great many patrons sought out the innkeeper to express their amusement at his radio advertising.

ADDITIONAL ADVERTISING POSSIBILITIES

In addition to newspapers, magazines, TV, and radio, there is a wide variety of other possibilities for advertising. You may choose to purchase some advertising space in the local Chamber of Commerce or Board of Trade brochure. This ad usually buys membership into these local organizations as well, which can be a source of support to you and your community. You may try an ad in a trade magazine or specialty publication geared to your particular clientele.

You will, undoubtedly, receive many requests for advertising from local non-profit service organizations. You will have to evaluate each request on its own merits. But if your advertising budget has been committed for the current year, invite people to contact you next year, at which time you will consider including them in your advertising budget. Of course, supporting your local organizations is certainly an aspect of being involved in your community; however, the demands can become a bit overwhelming. One effective way to cut down on the number of requests made by well-meaning local programs such as basketball or Little League championships, fairs, and the like, is to suggest you would be happy to contribute a small amount of money; however, the ad should be signed simply: "Compliments of a friend." This allows you to support the organization, but at the same time does not give your name as a prospect for other programs.

We have spent a long time writing about advertising because it is a major factor in doing business. We subscribe to a generalist definition of advertising as including anything you do which is directly observed by the public, whether you pay for it or not. The sign that you post on your front lawn is advertising. The pink and white petunias we plant in the flower beds are advertising (color recognition again). The vanity license plate "BRAMBL" which we purchase each year for the sports car (no, not pink or green)—too, is advertising. The meticulous care given to the buildings and grounds is advertising. If you are conscious of the advertising value of these elements, you will find more and more creative ways to advertise, to stretch your budget, and to help your business grow to success.

PUBLICITY

The very best way to get your story told is through publicity, which doesn't have a price tag, and is dependent only on your own ingenuity and your ability to generate news in and around your inn. You, of course, will consider everything you are doing in creating your country inn to be "newsworthy"! Not everything—but some things—will also be considered newsworthy by news media in your area.

The Bramble Inn has received excellent news coverage in the various media during the past six years, beginning the first season with two feature stories on the uniqueness of two women opening a country inn. Each year we write several news releases describing the major artists and their work exhibited at the gallery. The topics about your inn might be human interest stories or business news briefs. But your business will have a public impact and be of interest to the consumers of local media.

WRITING A NEWS RELEASE

Newspapers often will not be able to send a reporter to cover a local story, but if you mail a typewritten, double-spaced news release (see sample news release on page 124) telling who, what, when, where, and why, then you have a very good chance of getting your story in print—and at no cost to you except time and typewriter paper. Always try to send a glossy, black-and-white photograph along with the news release. Newspapers like to print good photos—they make a story more eye-appealing and, hence, readable.

GETTING YOUR INN READY TO OPEN

NEWS RELEASE

K. L. Etsell
Route 6A Box 159
Brewster, Mass. 02631

CONTACT: Karen L. Etsell
896-7644

                                         FOR IMMEDIATE RELEASE

Brewster, Mass. -- SIDEWALK PAINTING DEMONSTRATION. Foster H. Nystrom, nationally recognized painter in watercolor, will demonstrate how this fascinating medium performs during an outdoor show under the trees at THE BRAMBLE INN GALLERY AND CAFE on Wednesday, July 11th, from 11:30 to 1:30 P.M. THE BRAMBLE INN GALLERY is located on Route 6A in Brewster Center and off-street parking is available at the rear of the cafe.

      Mr. Nystrom studied at the Massachusetts College of Art and Pratt Institute and has painted much of the American and Austrian landscape with emphasis more recently on New England and especially Cape Cod. J.J. Powers writes, "Mr. Nystrom is a watercolorist who uses his media with the understanding of a trained outdoorsman, skier, and observer of the world around him. With the skill of the schooled perfectionist and the keen eye, his paintings present us with a view that is at once inspirational and refreshing."

      In case of rain, the demonstration will be held on Friday, July 13, from 11:30 to 1:30 P.M. An exhibit of Mr. Nystrom's paintings will continue on view at THE BRAMBLE INN GALLERY AND CAFE, Tuesday through Sunday, 11:30 to 8:30 P.M.

Sample News Release
(Fold in thirds so top half is seen immediately by editor)

Getting Your Story Told

It is essential to know the copy deadline dates for each newspaper in order to have your news release included in the right publication date. Otherwise your release may be published too soon or not at all.

You can send the same release to multiple sources, but don't send a poor reproduction copy or carbon copy. No news editor wants to think he or she is in the business of printing carbon copy news items. Also, be sure to send only newsworthy items. If you glut the mails with releases which have little real news interest, the editor will soon discount even the important information you send.

The personal touch is also important. Take time to stop by and introduce yourself to your local newspaper editor. Be polite and well-organized when dealing with the advertising sales agent who will visit you for an advertising account. You share a common consumer constituency with the local media and are in a position to work effectively together for mutual benefit.

After a while, you will become familiar with the kind of story preferred by each local media source. Use that knowledge to tailor-make the news release to fit the needs of each editor. Don't hesitate to make suggestions for special feature stories about an upcoming major event at your inn or request to be included in a special column. You have to become your own public relations person in order to keep your name in front of the public as much as possible. Rather than erring on the side of being too "pushy," most innkeepers tend to be so busy that opportunities for excellent news coverage are overlooked. If you are vigilant and professional in your approach, you should be able to obtain a great deal of publicity for relatively little expense.

It is here that your choice of a special focus for your inn will prove to be invaluable. As mentioned earlier, the antique glass conservatory at the Nauset House earned the attention of *Bride's* magazine, and many publications have done features on inns that have completed beautiful restorations of Victorian buildings, like the Mainstay in New Jersey, and the National House Inn in Michigan. Again, *location* comes up: a unique feature in your location, such as being on the bird-migration flyway or near a whale-watching point, will be of interest to the media.

TRAVEL GUIDES

Another source of publicity which is available to country innkeepers are the inn travel guide books and inn cookbooks which are published each year. The publisher requests permission to include details about your inn in his travel guide—or one of your favorite recipes in his inn cookbook—and then sells the book to the ever-increasing number of people who enjoy staying at country inns. Some guides are more selective than others and provide more up-to-date information. Over the years, travelers learn to know which guides are the most reliable.

The first and foremost of such country inn travel guides, *Country Inns and Back Roads,* is now in its sixteenth consecutive year of publication. Each year it is rewritten and revised by Norman Simpson, "The Berkshire Traveller," and is generally acclaimed as the grandfather of all country inn guides. Norman develops a close, personal relationship with the innkeepers of all the inns included in his book. Because he personally invites an inn to be included in *Country Inns and Back Roads*—which has a dedicated following—there is a mutual reliance on each other to do one's part well. The book is widely read because Norman is able to capture people's preferences for traveling experience and people have learned to trust his recommendations.

Inns included in *Country Inns and Back Roads* all are members of the Independent Innkeepers Association which is an informal and at the same time very effective loose confederation of keepers of country inns. It was founded the year after *Country Inns and Back Roads* was first published and has been continuing ever since. We attend overnight regional meetings, and also national three-day meetings which very frequently have foreign guest-innkeepers of inns included in *Country Inns and Back Roads, Britain and Ireland* and *Country Inns and Back Roads, Europe.* Since there are many common concerns, problems, and needs among innkeepers, the association enables the sharing of new ideas and support among likeminded people.

We wrote to Norman and invited him to visit The Bramble Inn when he came to Cape Cod. On his first visit, he agreed that our inn was a rather unique place. He carefully explained that he was interested in inviting into the association and the book only those innkeepers who were enthusiastic about sharing ideas and goals. There has been a great deal of communication ever since and it has been a most happy experience for us.

GUEST TV APPEARANCES

Although the written word has provided the most consistent news coverage for our inn, we have found TV, in particular, to have a phenomenally strong impact on public behavior. The largest number of diners ever to come to The Bramble Inn arrived the night after Karen's first TV guest appearance on "Women '78," a program focusing on the varied activities of women in New England. We had written a letter directly to the show's producer to tell about our business enterprise and were invited to appear on the program. Karen displayed some of the artwork for sale in the gallery, prepared gazpacho soup, and talked with the show's hostess, Sharon King, about being an innkeeper/businesswoman on Cape Cod. Four years later, loyal viewers are still stopping Karen at the inn to tell her they saw her on the TV! An appearance on TV becomes a news release on its own merit to local newspapers, since local people want to know who among them can be seen on TV. So one television appearance can generate a great deal of free exposure for your country inn.

There is no need to stop at one TV appearance either. If you are persistent and lucky, you may even find a TV program which needs a regular segment such as "resident chef." If you enjoy being on TV, a regular appearance could do wonders for the reputation of your inn's dining room.

PROMOTION

As you go along in business month by month, you will want to keep an eye out for opportunities to promote your country inn. These opportunities will help to insure that your business will be reading on the black side of the ledger as soon as possible. A good advertising campaign is one way to promote your business, and usually involves some form of public announcement through the use of media, by printed matter or by TV or radio broadcasts. Promotion includes advertising and publicity, but is really much broader in scope. By definition, promotion literally means "to move forward, to elevate, to advance." It means "to contribute to the growth or prosperity of something." There are many, many creative avenues by which you can be the successful promoter of your business.

BUSINESS AND TRADE ORGANIZATIONS

One of the first promotional activities you should be involved in is to join your local community Board of Trade or Chamber of Commerce. This will give your new business visibility and support within the local business community. Remember: "business brings business." The healthier the business climate is in your community, the easier it will be for your business to succeed. So it behooves you to join and attend meetings of your local business organization. It is also a great way to spread the news about what you are doing. You need this network of other business people—and they need you!

You may also choose to join other business or trade organizations which promote the goals closely identified with yours, such as the regional and national hotel and restaurant associations. Through these avenues, you will be able to take an active role in promoting the industry of which you are a part, and through which your business will benefit from your extended reputation. It is wise, however, to make sure that the "home fires" are being well-tended while you are away. Your business can benefit by this organizational work only if it is running smoothly without you. You can benefit a great deal both personally and professionally by becoming active in your state and local trade organizations. If you choose to join, but cannot actively participate, you can still benefit by attending selected seminars, workshops, and trade shows. The organizations publish pamphlets and magazines which keep you current with news affecting legislation, new product lines, and other factors affecting your business.

NEW PRODUCT DEVELOPMENTS

Another excellent way to promote your business is to develop a specialized product that will be identified with your inn. A great example of this is the Toll House cookie, created during World War II at the Toll House Inn in Whitman, Massachusetts! At the Bramble Inn we have developed an original recipe for a cranberry dessert pastry which we call the Cape Cod Bramble. We serve the Cape Cod Bramble in our own restaurant and we also sell it as an over-the-counter bakery item. During the past six years, we have also marketed the Cape Cod Bramble to other restaurants in the area. Since it has the regional appeal of the cranberry (Cape Cod is famous for its many cranberry bogs!) and it can only be produced by The Bramble Inn, the dessert has become an item totally identified with our business.

Write a Cookbook — Another product we developed which has promoted the reputation of The Bramble Inn is our own cookbook. We collected all of our best recipes, including old family favorites and nearly all the recipes that we serve at the inn (with the exception of the Cape Cod Bramble, of course!). We wrote the book and published it during our second year in business in response to the many requests we had for our recipes. Now, whenever we have such requests, we can proudly offer the cookbook for sale to anyone interested.

In keeping with our theme, we hand-lettered the recipes and used original sketches for illustration throughout the cookbook. We published it locally and it is now in its second expanded printing. To enhance the promotion of the inn through the cookbook, we have distributed it wholesale to several bookstores in New England. In order to obtain an even wider market, we placed a mail-order ad in a national magazine. Our goal for the cookbook was really twofold. We wanted, of course, to make a profit on its sale. More important was its promotional value, since the sale of each cookbook would bring the name of our inn into a large number of households throughout the country.

Several inns have utilized the cookbook idea: Nora McNab Moyse in Washington has just published her Partridge Inn cookbook; and among others who have been doing their own cookbooks for years are the Nu-Wray Inn in North Carolina; the Beaumount Inn, the Inn at Pleasant Hill, and the Boone Tavern in Kentucky; and the Cheshire Inn in Missouri.

Develop Your Own Product — There are numerous ideas for product development that would provide good promotional value for your country inn. These are the ones we developed, but your imagination will help you find ones particularly suited to your business. For instance, the Chalet Suzanne in Florida was famous for its exceptional soups. So they developed a line of canned soups which they market throughout the country. Now people can enjoy those wonderful Florida flavors when they are sitting down for dinner in Duluth! And the reputation of the Chalet Suzanne goes everywhere their canned soups go—which is a far distance!

In developing a product, you have to have patience, creativity, and determination. So many good ideas remain just that—good ideas. But turning one good idea into a successful product is worth all the energy it takes to do it.

Service Marks and Trademarks — In order to protect the name "Bramble" that we were working hard to promote, it was important to obtain service marks and trademarks for this purpose. As long as no one else has been granted a "service mark" on the same name, you can easily obtain a state and federal service mark which protects the name of your business establishment. A patent lawyer is the best professional suited to help you obtain this protection.

Obtaining a registered federal trademark on a product such as our dessert pastry is quite complicated and time-consuming. The state trademark can be obtained relatively easily, but it does not offer any protection to your product outside the state. Therefore, the federal trademark is the essential mark to obtain. Again, the assistance of a patent lawyer is most helpful. If you can prove that you have a unique product or name—and if no one else has registered a trademark on the same item—the trademark will be issued and will provide you with a great deal of protection for your production and marketing effort of the product. And the more widely you are able to promote the product, the more well-known your inn will become.

SPECIAL EVENTS

You can generate interest in your inn and garner

widespread publicity by developing your own special events.

We have arranged special events in order to bring The Bramble Inn into the public view, especially when we reopen each spring, to remind people that we are still here. These events have been luncheon fashion shows with Lily Pulitzer clothing, sidewalk watercolor painting demonstrations, scrimshaw demonstrations—all with news releases to several local newspapers and magazines to assure good news coverage of the events.

Special events can be organized around holidays— Paul Pearson at the Maryland Inn holds a Halloween Freakers' Ball and a Dickens Christmas; "sugaring-off" parties are an annual spring rite at the Handfield Inn in Quebec; at the Inn at Huntington in Massachusetts, special chamber and choral music is performed throughout the Christmas season. There are many other kinds of special events various inn have instituted: Sunday concerts are held at the Old Rittenhouse Inn in Wisconsin; Stafford's in the Field in New Hampshire holds Saturday night square dances in their huge barn; and the Lodge on the Desert in Arizona features birdwatching tours conducted by expert ornithologists.

YOUR GREATEST PROMOTIONAL RESOURCE

In addition to any special products you might develop, you must remember to promote your greatest and most valuable resource to its utmost. That resource is YOU! Remember that people are interested to know *who* you are and what *you* are doing. Keep the local news media informed of anything you do that is newsworthy— whether or not it is directly related to your business. Chances are the name of your business will be printed in the paper along with any use of your name. Be conscious of your activities and interests and the promotional value they hold for your business.

If you take a trip to France, for instance, to become more familiar with French cooking and the wonderful continental culinary traditions, incorporate that into a news release upon your return. Your clientele will want to know that they can look forward to some European flair in your country inn! Or if you are invited to submit one of your recipes for a new cookbook about to be published on country inn cooking, be sure to send a news release about this to your local media. These kinds of honors should not pass by unheralded! All the while, your business will be gaining in reputation, stability and profits.

There are many, many ways to promote your business which you will discover as you go along. Choose those that best fit your style and objectives. You might consider writing a weekly column on food or cooking for your local newspaper. That way, you can keep your name once again in the public spotlight. Perhaps hosting civic events such as the Rotary's weekly luncheon or the garden club's annual banquet will be a good promotional tool. Holding wedding receptions might add a nice element to your business and introduce your inn to people who might otherwise not have an opportunity to visit you.

Perhaps speaking to small groups of interested people on "Innkeeping" or "The Joys of Owning Your Own Business" would be just the thing for you! Sharing information you have that others want is a great way to promote your business.

It is important to tell people about significant events at your inn and remind them why they should come for a visit. Don't hide your light under a basket! You must be an assertive optimist when seeking news coverage. If you remember you are doing a *service* for others by sharing yourself and your story, you will be less hesitant to ask for such exposure.

PART III

Operating A Successful Country Inn

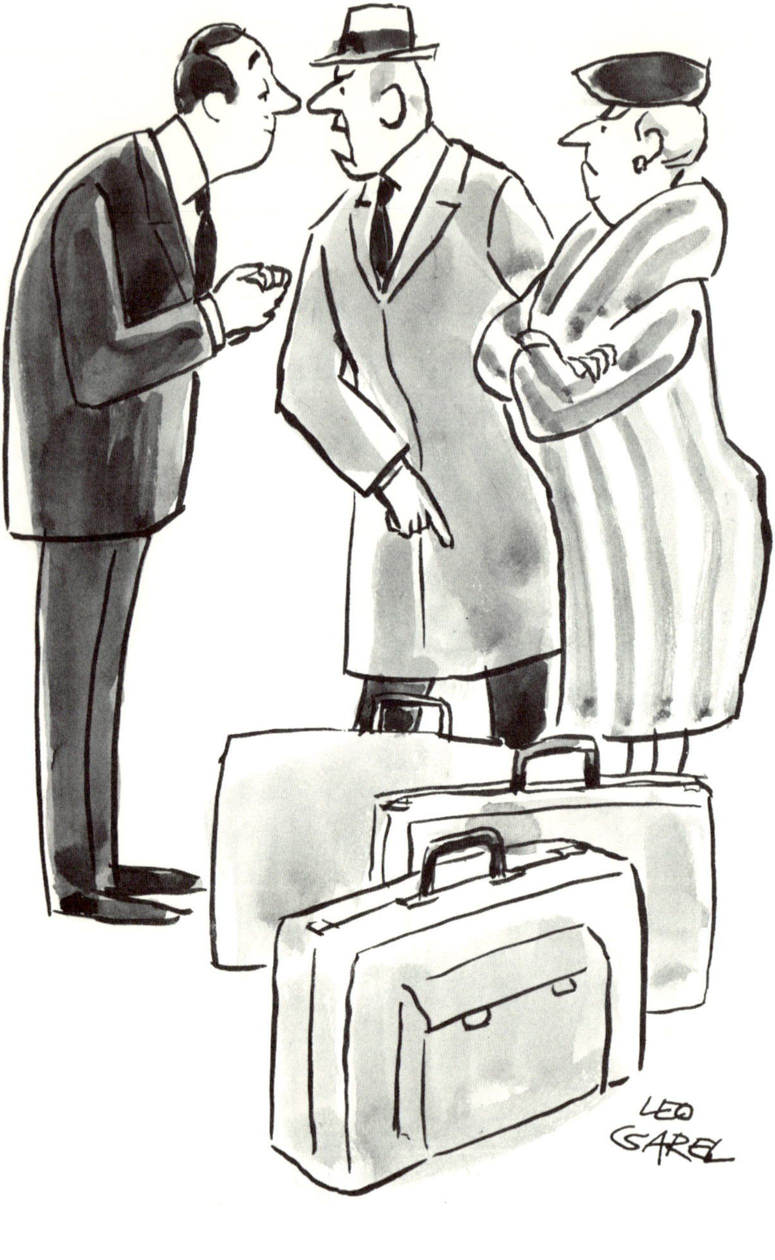
LEO GAREL

12
BASIC OPERATING PROCEDURES

There are certain invariables in innkeeping just as there are in any business. Although an innkeeper's day is filled with variety—no two days are the same—there is a daily schedule to be followed (for an exact breakdown of ours, see page 158). A typical sixteen-hour day starts at 8:00 A.M. and usually ends around 11:30 P.M., with perhaps a fifteen-minute break for breakfast and a half-hour break for dinner.

Usually from 9:00 A.M. to 11:30 P.M. there are employees to schedule, direct, and supervise. The phone rings demandingly throughout the day. Salespeople arrive and require your attention. At least one delivery usually presents a problem. For instance, the ice-cream truck with the noisy refrigeration system makes its delivery at 12:30 P.M. during your busiest lunchtime!

Guests are delighted finally to arrive at your lovely country inn and want to have a leisurely chat with you about the joys of the quiet life style of a country innkeeper. And the beat goes on . . . ! No one task in the day of an innkeeper is too demanding by itself. But the cumulative effect of these diverse requirements makes for a hectic and stimulating day. And then comes the Fourth of July weekend when your commercial hot water heater springs a leak and you try to reschedule your day somehow to handle the crisis!

INNKEEPER-GUEST RELATIONSHIPS

Assuming that you like people and enjoy having guests, your relationship with your guests will be pleasant and rewarding. There are a few areas, however, that deserve a few words of advice.

Sometimes—no matter how lovely your facilities are or how gracious your service—there will be guests who have complaints. It is best to listen to all your guests' comments and suggestions. Acknowledge that you are sorry when they are displeased or uncomfortable, evaluate the merits of the complaint, make any improvement that seems necessary, and then go about your business as usual.

It is a good idea to keep in mind the saying, "You can't please all of the people all of the time . . . " There is the rare occasion when no matter what you do, it isn't going to be enough. Larry Hyde recounts the time a family of five arrived without a reservation at the Inn on the Library Lawn, and he went all out to accommodate them in one single and one double room, moving in a crib, a mattress, all the necessary linens, and complimentary beverages for all. An hour later, he stopped by to see how they were faring, and found the following note: "Because there is no television in the room, the library clock (one block away) is too loud, the dining room is downstairs, breakfast won't be available until 7:00 A.M. and the room was not air conditioned, we have gone to find a Holiday Inn. Here is $2 for your effort." Larry, in the prescribed manner for all innkeepers, took it in stride, saying simply, "Some people are country inn people, and some people are not."

Every so often you turn a potentially disastrous situation into a positive experience for you and your guests. Late one evening recently two guests arrived at the inn to register for their room. They apologized for arriving so late and we told them we were sorry but we did not have them registered with us and that we had no more vacancies. However, rather than turn them away, we invited them in and tried to help find them lodging that night elsewhere. As the minutes went by, the guests realized they had confused the dates and they had reserved accommodations at another inn several miles away. They did, indeed, have a room reserved with us the following night. They quickly went along to the other inn for the night and happily returned to us the following day, very appreciative of our hospitality.

There are wonderful stories of guests who never utter a word of complaint under the most trying circumstances. Margie Alcarese at the Wayside Inn in Virginia has the most warming memories of a night during a snowstorm when it seemed everything that could go wrong, did—the electricity was knocked out on a *literally* overflow crowd waiting for tables in the dining rooms. The waiting guests spilled over into every conceivable space, including hallways and stairways. As if that weren't enough, a few hours later (after the electricity had been restored), there was a breakdown in the town water system, and they had no water for five hours. This meant that in addition to no hot water, there was no heat!

Earlier, when all the lights had gone out, Margie made the rounds, reassuring the guests that candlelight and firelight in the fireplaces would evoke the spirit of 1797 (the original date of the Wayside Inn), and she was most impressed by the calmness and serenity with which everyone responded to the emergency; some guests even tried to assist in locating the problem. When the water was shut off, some of the staff who had property with well water formed a water brigade, bringing in enough water to wash some dishes and supply the needy bar! The guests, with extra blankets and the few electric heaters that could be found, endured admirably. Margie says she will never forget the way everyone rose to the occasion with humor and understanding, turning a potential disaster into a warm and congenial experience.

Another kind of story is told by Betsy Guido at the Chester Inn in Vermont, and here it is in her words: "During a quiet time when there were few guests expected, the chambermaids took advantage of the opportunity to do a major cleaning of the third-floor rooms. They stripped the rooms of linens, bedding, curtains, and even removed the furniture in order to clean the rugs.

"It was also a perfect time to hire a new 'front desk' person. There would be plenty of time to give her good training without too many interruptions. We did, however, make one major mistake. Because it was so quiet we never thought to mark the third-floor rooms 'Hold' in the reservation book.

"Through the front door walked two gentlemen looking for a bargain. Our second-floor rooms were 'too expensive.' Didn't we have something cheaper? Totally unaware of our third-floor situation, our new receptionist smiled politely and sent them up the stairs for their less costly room.

"We never heard a word from them. All of us were oblivious to what had taken place until later the next morning when the chambermaids reported that someone had spent the night in Room 18! Our overnight guests, looking for a bargain, spent the night in a room on mattresses with no sheets or blankets, no towels with which to shower or bathe, no curtains to keep out the morning light. Smiling, they paid their bill in the early morning, said they'd had a lovely time and they'd be back." Sometimes it takes so little to make people happy.

The ultimate story of the uncomplaining guest has to be the incident at the Redcoat's Return in the Catskills. Peggy Wright prided herself on the fact that bolts and locks were unnecessary in their "crimeless" inn, and had never bothered with having keys made for the bedroom doors. She had found a batch of old skeleton keys (circa 1910) which she had kept but never used. These could, if need be, work interchangeably in any and all the locks. On one particularly quiet evening, the only guests to arrive for the night were a couple of newlyweds who were beginning their two-week honeymoon with their first country inn experience. After registering they discreetly requested a key. Peggy rather resignedly explained keys weren't really necessary, but picked a key at random from her antique collection and gave it to them. The couple retired happily to their room, locking the door behind them. Peggy describes the events of the next day as they unfolded:

"The following morning at eight o'clock, Tom and I stood by in the kitchen, ready to prepare a robust breakfast for our newlyweds. As the morning wore on—ten o'clock came and went—we became increasingly restless, anxious to get on with the many chores awaiting us. Finally at noon, Tom looked at me quizzically and suggested that I go up into the hotel and try to determine if anyone was moving about. I hesitated, as I didn't want to intrude on their privacy; however, we *were* tired of standing around waiting and wondering in the kitchen. So, I approached the staircase on tiptoe and began a silent ascent to the third floor. As I rounded the first flight of stairs, I froze in my tracks upon hearing a shrill and desperate voice crying, 'Help!' Fearing some hideous domestic quarrel, I hesitated, undecided.

"'Please, someone—HELP!' The tired, helpless tone of this new plea galvanized me into action, and I raced up the final flight. There before me, half-hanging out of the open transom over their bedroom door, was the frantic face of the young bride. I was aghast at her disheveled state. When she saw me, she sighed, 'Thank God!'

"'We've broken the key off in the lock and can't get out,' she wearily explained. The only alternative exit was a forty-foot leap to the porch roof two stories below. I quickly assured her we would get another key and attempt to open the door from the outside. After a nervous half hour of Tom's working at it, the broken-off key was finally pushed out of the lock, clanking on the floor when it fell. Release at last!

"From inside the quiet room, a weary voice asked pathetically, 'Can we still have breakfast?'"

That request was only too happily fulfilled. But innkeepers quickly learn that people will have a *wide* range of requests about which it is best to have set a firm policy beforehand. For example, if you do not allow pets, you must specify this in your brochure and be consistent about enforcing the policy. If one guest leaves his favorite puppy home and sees some other "man's best friend" in the hallway, you will have a justifiably angry guest asking to see the manager.

Pet stories are many, and the Baileys at the Grey Whale Inn in California have one of a more unusual variety. When a family with two boys was finally preparing to leave, well past checkout time, and the maid was coming in to the room with the vacuum to get on with her delayed cleaning, the boys said, "Oh, don't vacuum in our room— our snakes got loose and we can't find them!" Needless to say, this threw the entire inn staff and management into an uproar. It seems that the boys had caught two garter snakes and smuggled them into their rooms and then let them get away. The snakes seemed to have vanished, until the next day, when one of them was spied and captured as it was making its way up the stairs. The second snake has not been seen since. Hopefully, it has quietly removed itself from the premises. The moral to this story, the Baileys say, is that anything can (and probably will) happen in August.

POLICY FOR LODGING RESERVATIONS

One of the first operational decisions you will make

for your inn is your policy for accepting advanced reservations and cancellations for lodging accommodations. There are almost as many variations on this theme as there are in a good piece of jazz. In deciding on the policy which was best for us, we reviewed the policies of several well-run inns in the area. We came up with the following set of procedures which has worked very well for us over the years.

For a one-night stay, we ask for one night's lodging as the deposit for advanced reservations. For a two- to four-night stay, we require a two-night deposit. For longer than four nights, we require fifty percent of the entire stay. The deposit is applied to the last night's stay, should guests decide to leave early. We allow approximately five days for the check to arrive in the mail, and encourage people to send off their deposits immediately. Our philosophy is: we commit one of our rooms to a guest and the guest is equally committed to us for the length of his or her stay— barring an unforeseen emergency, of course. If guests are seriously intending to keep their reservations, they are quite willing to comply immediately with your deposit requirements. We do not accept credit card reservations by phone, since the cardholder is under no obligation to pay for the accommodations if he does not keep them. We will gladly refund a deposit if cancellation notice is received at least two weeks before the date of arrival.

From time to time we do have guests who are reluctant to send a deposit because, "what if the weather isn't any good?" or some such reason. Those are the chances that guests and innkeepers have to take together since innkeepers don't have control over the weather—yet! If your policy is not tight enough, you will find that you are having many "no-shows," unexpectedly empty rooms, and—even worse—overbooking, all of which are bad signs for an innkeeping business.

Another question often asked is, "When should a guest pay for the remainder of his stay?" Our policy is: Pay at the time of check-in and registration. Again, a guest has requested that you reserve a room, perhaps for four days in the middle of your busiest season. He has sent you the required two-night deposit. Is he committed to pay you for the last two days' stay? Of course, he is! Before you give possession of your room to your guest, he should live up to his part of the commitment upon arrival and pay for the last two nights' stay. Then everyone's expectations have been met and guest and innkeeper can go about their business enjoying each other's presence.

Some innkeepers do choose to run a tab for accommodations, meals, and other services as large hotels do, to be paid at checkout time. This may work for some establishments, but the risk of early departure and lost revenues is much greater than collecting fees "up front."

For those occasions when someone wants to squeeze an extra person into a lodging room, you will need to have a policy about accommodating extra guests in your inn rooms. Some guests are happy to pay for the extra person and some just want to have free accommodations. We always confirm the number of people expected when taking a reservation. We explain that because of the fire laws covering such an old house, we are limited in our license to sleeping only one or two people in a room. We do not have cots or cribs available to add to the rooms. Sometimes this means that we are unable to accommodate certain guests, but it is our way of limiting the use of the inn rooms to either double or single occupancy.

CREDIT CARDS

The use of credit cards seems to have become an accepted part of our society. Especially when people are travelling, they hesitiate to carry large amounts of cash. When an establishment accepts credit cards, it becomes a service to the guests. The bankers' theory, of course, holds that people are likely to spend more money when they can use their credit cards. The disadvantage to the innkeeper is that you have to pay a percentage of your gross receipts charged to the credit cards. At least a portion of the general public does not realize this. It is illegal, however, to charge the credit card purchaser any more for the service than is charged to a cash customer. Also, when customers put tips on the credit cards, you have to pay for that charge as well. We ask diners if they would kindly leave the tip at the table for the waitress rather than put the tip on the charge card. We do accept credit cards as payment for all our services.

"SERVICE WITH A SMILE"

In addition to these policy and operational decisions involved with the business side of innkeeper-guest relations, there are the human interactions which are completely unpredictable, requiring action above and beyond the call of duty. As, for instance, the incident involving a gentleman guest at the Mainstay Inn who was discovered at midnight sleepwalking all through the house, upstairs and down—naked. He had filled a sink with water in an unoccupied room before Tom Carroll managed to herd him back into his room. No mention was made of the incident the following morning, and the gentleman probably doesn't know to this day of his midnight stroll.

As you've probably gathered by now, every inn has a collection of stories about the interesting, funny, kind, wonderful people who cross their thresholds, as well as a few difficult, irascible, and impossible ones. A sense of humor can get you over a lot of rough spots. In general, if you remember the old adage "Service with a smile," you will get through even the most uncomfortable situations. Saying, "I'm sorry," never hurts when you are in the public service business. Your guests may be tired and hassled and even curt from a long day's drive. It is important to treat everyone as graciously as you would like to be treated.

This, after all, is the heart of country innkeeping—offering warm and personal hospitality which makes guests feel special and happy to be with us.

MAINTAINING YOUR COUNTRY INN

One of the least glamorous but most visible tasks you will perform is the development of a regular maintenance program for your property. This will include the day-to-day care of your buildings and grounds, as well as the periodic repairs and renovations required to keep the property in tip-top condition. Any homeowner knows the constant requirements for care and maintenance which go along with owning property. Those big and small requirements are multiplied many times over when your property is a large "home away from home" for many people. Just imagine how many leaky faucets need to be repaired over a five-year period in a big old inn with numerous lodging rooms and baths!

PLAN A MAINTENANCE PROGRAM

Your guests expect your country inn to be well-maintained. Cleanliness and attention to details do count. Clean grout between bathroom tiles is noticed. The best way to keep your inn well-maintained is to plan your maintenance program ahead over a period of years. This will include plans for such things as new painting inside and out, wallpapering, floors, cracked ceilings, outside shutters, new gravel for driveway, expanded landscaping, and leaky roof repairs. If you make projections and have repairs done periodically, then everything doesn't fall apart at the same time. You can spread your expenses over a period of years which is a tax benefit to you as a business expense. The periodic replacement of such supplies and equipment as old beds and mattresses, worn sheets and towels, and faded carpets has to be figured into your maintenance expense program, too.

The trick is to have any repairs done just *before* people begin to notice that they need to be done. Arrange to have the new coat of paint applied just before the chipping of the old paint is noticeable. If your inn is large or if you are short of funds, plan to stagger any major repairs. For example, paint the most visible half of the building one year. Then finish the second half the next year when you have more funds available.

As an innkeeper you will need to know how to do many minor repairs yourself unless you want to pay astronomical service charges for incidental problems. For a person who likes to putter and fix things, being an innkeeper is an ideal profession. If you get a lot of satisfaction from figuring out how to replace a loose O-ring in a leaky faucet, you will probably be a happy innkeeper! Innkeeping is full of instances which provide a sense of accomplishment—small and large—and mastery over the environment.

KEEPING ACCURATE RECORDS IS GOOD BUSINESS

There are two reasons why good records must be kept—for legal purposes and as management tools. Certain legal records are required by the government to be preserved for a specified number of years. These records deal mostly with personnel-payroll data and income tax figures. Your accountant can tell you which records need to be retained for what length of time. Other legal papers should also be retained such as proof of ownership, copyrights, leases, corporation bylaws, and annual reports.

For use as a management tool, a good accounting system which you can understand and use easily should be set up. I have noted previously the importance of developing monthly budgets and cost comparisons. This system will help you to analyze, plan, set goals, follow up, and even borrow money when and if you need to. Journals, ledgers, accounts payable, accounts receivable, and a petty cash fund are all part of this record-keeping system which will enable you to know how much business you are doing at any given time.

As the owner of an inn, you will also want to keep a guest book for registration and another one for other visitors to sign and leave comments if they wish. You can use this to develop an effective mailing list for holiday greeting cards, new brochures, other reminders or promotional material for your inn, and even as a mail order mailing list should you develop some items that you would like to sell. By using this mailing list, you can remind former guests and visitors about your inn and encourage them to return for another visit soon.

Storage of records is a continual problem in terms of both space and accessibility. Beyond the records required to be kept by law, you will decide which other records to keep and how long to keep them, according to your own experience. You will find shortly which records you must keep easily accessible and which ones can go into the rear of the back closet. A four-drawer file cabinet has proven to be an indispensable part of our office over the years. Storing older records systematically in well-labeled corrugated boxes is usually a good method to follow. Some larger businesses choose to store their important records on microfilm.

The last caution about record-keeping is the importance of planning for record retention in the event of a disaster, such as a flood, fire, earthquake, or hurricane. If a disaster should strike, you will need to have records which will allow you to re-establish your business, collect insurance, report losses for income tax purposes, and borrow money. The most important disaster records might be the most recent annual profit and loss statement, balance sheet, and income tax return. In planning against a disaster, you might keep a duplicate set of these records in two different locations. A fire-resistant safe on the premises is helpful, as well. Some people choose to keep a disaster file in storage in a bank safe-deposit box (the fee for which is tax deductible). Wherever you store your disaster records, be sure to review the file periodically to make certain that you have entered the most up-to-date summaries of your business.

In other sections of this book, I have commented on the advisability of keeping records in connection with various aspects of innkeeping. Careful filing of warranties, service instructions, and model numbers for appliances, and other similar papers or information is most important. There are all kinds of records and information which need to be kept in the operation of a restaurant or gift shop, or any other enterprises that are a part of your inn. I need not stress the importance of keeping an up-to-date telephone book. By allocating space in advance, whether it is in a file cabinet, a box, a folder, or an envelope, for the many types of records you must keep, you will be contributing in no small measure to the smooth operation of your country inn.

13

EXPANSION AND GROWTH

CAPITALIZE ON YOUR THEME

After you open your country inn and get the lodging accommodations and restaurant off the ground and functioning well, you can turn your attention to developing other aspects of your business which will expand upon your existing theme. Some of these expansion ideas could include opening a gift or antique shop or a handcraft shop. You might offer ski-tour packages in the winter or rent sailboats from your lakefront dock. You could arrange hayrides in the fall or tours of California wineries. Your choice, of course, will depend on your location and your own interests.

ON RUNNING AN ART GALLERY

We chose to open the art gallery as a natural extension of our interests and a place to show our own work, as well as the works of fifteen to twenty local and off-Cape, artists. Throughout the summer, we send prepared weekly news releases to local newspapers to tell the public about the work of artists currently showing at the gallery.

Reviewers for art columns visit the gallery from time to time to cover the exhibitions as well.

Finding new artwork is one of the very pleasant off-season tasks that we relish doing. We are always on the lookout for new local talent. We attend artists' receptions and visit local shows throughout the winter. Cape Cod has a very active winter artist population and the time spent at these exhibits, seeing new artists' work, is enjoyable. Also, whenever we travel, we try to visit galleries and attend art openings to see local talent. In short, we are always looking for new artists to include in the gallery in order to provide a stimulating environment for our patrons.

There are many restaurants which decorate their walls with art work. Some even offer the paintings for sale. There is a vast difference in *purpose,* however, from that kind of art display and the actual art gallery environment at The Bramble Inn. The difference has mostly to do with the commitment and serious intent in promoting the art gallery as a separate complement to the rest of the inn and café!

There are many "tips" that we have learned over the years of running the gallery. Keep a guest book so you can send out mailings for special events or shows. Don't negotiate the price of a piece of art. If the artist has indicated his price and the customer appreciates the artist's work—and if the price is a fair one to begin with—the customer should be willing to pay. We show only framed pieces because they present themselves so much better that way. Obtain a brochure or biographical sketch from each artist. Buyers like to know about the artist who created the work hanging in their homes or offices; the purchase of a piece of art is a very personal one. Lastly, keep accurate records of the artwork you receive from artists and on the pieces you sell. Pay commissions promptly and keep duplicate lists of work received and returned, signed by you and the artist.

ON RUNNING A GIFT SHOP

In keeping with the art gallery theme, we also have a gift shop which specializes in handcrafted gifts. Many of these gifts are truly art forms in themselves. We have jewelry, unique stationery, antique hand-crocheted bedspreads, tablecloths, napkins, doilies, pottery, and the like. The gifts are especially selected to complement the art gallery environment. Even the homemade jelly that we sell has a little calico cap added to make it a delightful gift.

There are several national and regional gift shows for the wholesale trade held throughout the year. Distributors for all the lines of traditional giftware are represented at these gift shows. They are fascinating to attend. The gifts represented are for the mass market, however, rather than the unique one-of-a-kind gifts you can obtain directly from the craftsperson. Depending on the kind of gifts you wish to carry in your gift shop, you may want to attend one of the gift trade shows in your area.

With a clientele that appreciates more unique, handmade things you will probably be interested in showing handcrafted items in your shop, and you can have a wonderful time attending local and national craft shows. Every community usually has some kind of association of local craftspeople. With a little investigation you can find out where and when the shows are held and you will be able to purchase the works of local craftspeople. If you have the time and inclination, you can plan to attend one of the larger regional crafts shows, such as the one held each summer in Rhinebeck, New York. This show attracts some of the finest craftspeople and artisans from all over New England. You would be certain to find many beautiful handmade items for your gift shop at such a show.

It is customary to sell gift items at a 100% markup over the wholesale price; for example, if an item costs you two dollars wholesale, it would sell for four dollars retail. With one-of-a-kind pieces of artwork, this percentage markup is usually too high. Most galleries charge a 40% commission fee to the artist; for example, if a painting sold for $100, the artist would receive $60 and the art gallery would receive $40. There are many exceptions to this 60/40 split, however. For example, we like to sell as many works as possible for the artists, so we choose to charge a lower gallery commission of 35%. This enables the retail price of the painting to be lower to encourage more sales.

Importing Gift Items — Shopping for unique items to sell or display at your establishment can become a complex undertaking. We found ourselves in the business of direct importers since we could not obtain a particular product any other way. The very first item we selected for our dining room tables—which became the centerpiece of the decor—was a lovely hand-painted pink, green, and white, flowered Italian napkin ring. We purchased the entire stock available at a large retail department store in Boston, intending to sell the extras to our gift shop customers. The response to the napkin rings was so positive the first year in business that we knew we needed to purchase many more dozen—hopefully, this time on a wholesale basis. Unfortunately, the department store had decided not to reorder the napkin rings and its stock was completely sold out. We spent several months contacting other large stores, gift shops, and wholesale gift distributors. Nobody had the napkin rings, or even anything closely resembling them. The only alternative we had was to write directly to the firm in Italy who manufactured them. After another several months of written communication with the firm in Italy (you think the U.S. Postal Service is slow!), we had received a very large supply of beautiful pink, green and white napkin rings. The written communications were done in English rather than Italian, and we had to pay for the shipment in U.S. dollars before they would ship it to us. At the end, there was a complicated matter of getting the shipment released from the foreign dock. This required the expensive services of a "customs broker."

Through this whole complicated transaction, it became clear that the wholesale importing of gifts (and other products as well) is a complex one. If you are involved in it on a daily basis, the labyrinth is probably quite understandable. But, otherwise, it is much easier to go to a wholesale distributor's warehouse or to a trade gift show to buy your giftwares. The percentage you pay to the wholesale importer now seems well worth the while after our importing experience! The exception, of course, is when you can *only* get what you want by arranging the deal yourself. In that case, it is all worth the effort and when we need a new supply of napkin rings, I'm sure we will again be in the import business!

The "Free Souvenirs" Problem — A good way to keep customers from walking away with "free souvenirs" from your inn rooms is to *sell* as many items as you can in your gift shop. We have some unusual appointments at each dining table which we announce, on a table tent, are for sale in the gift shop. They include individual glass salt and pepper cellars with glass spoons, the hand-painted Italian napkin rings, and decorative green bottle vases with pink dried flowers. These items would be difficult to find in a regular gift shop. People admire the items at their tables, and many wish to purchase them for their own homes or as gifts. If they were not available for sale in our gift shop, the temptation to pocket them might be great, indeed. As it is, we can count on two hands the number of thefts that have occurred during the past five years. It would be great if no one stole anything from public places, realizing that pilferage just boosts the price of the goods which is then passed along to the consumer. However, human nature being what it is, this seems to us like a tolerably low incidence of theft over the years.

Expansion and Growth

HOW WILL YOU GROW?

At some point in your successful innkeeping career, you will be confronted with the question of whether or not to expand your business. You may consider expansion because your business continues to increase and you know you could handle even more satisfied customers. Perhaps competition from other businesses in the area is making you consider expanding your own. Maybe your guests are requesting expansion of your lodging facilities or a larger dinner menu. Growth and expansion of an existing business can bring an exciting dimension to your business. But when it comes time to consider expanding, remember not to change just for change's sake. You have worked hard to present a product that people enjoy. Sometimes more is not necessarily better. If you add a large new wing with additional inn rooms, what will happen to your loyal guests who prefer your inn because of its small, quiet ambience? An important point to remember is that once you have developed a formula that works, *do not* change it! Repeat business is built on consistency. If you can manage to expand without changing that formula, keeping the service personal and gracious, perhaps your growth won't be objectionable to anyone.

If you finally decide to expand, you will begin by evaluating the expansion possibilities of your current location. Is there physical room to expand your facilities? Hopefully, you planned for success when you initially purchased your current property, and there is plenty of room to expand the physical plant. If not, your plans for growth still do not have to be shelved entirely. You could consider buying another piece of property nearby to renovate as an annex to your current country inn. Or you might be ready to sell your business completely and invest your earnings in a larger country inn in a completely new location. There you could experiment with your newly expanded business concepts. The pros and cons of expansion depend greatly on your own goals and objectives in life. If running a small country inn was your way of leaving the "rat race" of hectic corporate life, you should think twice before expanding your country inn business into a "rat race" of its own.

If you decide not to expand your country inn, you still have to deal with the issue of how to remain vibrant and committed to excellence over the years. Those innkeepers who continue to enjoy their work over a long career have found that there are enough rewards in innkeeping to warrent continuing in the business. They have etched out rewards that are essential to their happiness—perhaps money, good friends and acquaintances, travel, creativity, independence, and self-satisfaction rate high among them. If we don't continue to grow in some way, then we begin to stagnate. Growth can be achieved in such a wide variety of ways; it does not simply mean expanding into a larger facility, although that can be a meaningful objective for an ambitious innkeeper. However, growth in *some* form is essential to the successful country inn business.

HOW DO YOU JUDGE SUCCESS.

The day will arrive when you feel your country inn business is moving along very well, and you will take a deep breath and ask, "Am I a successful innkeeper yet?" How long you work before you can answer that question positively depends on many factors: What is your definition of success? Does success mean the ability to meet your monthly expenses and to have no cash-flow problem? Or does success mean taking an annual salary of $25,000 out of the business? Financial rewards may depend on the size of the capital investment you were able to make initially, how large your mortgage and other monthly carrying costs are, as well as what volume of business you are doing.

Or does success mean how happy you are with your

Expansion and Growth

chosen life style? How excited you are to greet the challenges of each new day? Are your energies being tapped in a creative and meaningful way? Success can be measured in many ways. It is up to each innkeeper to judge his or her success according to the factors which are important to him or her. Only you can judge how well the life style of innkeeper suits your needs for success.

* * *

Throughout this book we have progressed from the idea of becoming an innkeeper to the research and preparation, to the search for a property, to the acquisition of the inn, to putting the inn into operation and attracting guests, and finally, to keeping the inn going.

If you have read this far and are still excited about the prospects of owning and running a country inn, then we salute and encourage you to go ahead with your dreams. The spirit of innkeeping is contagious. It is a great way of life for those who have a combination of ambition, skill, patience, and creativity. It is not an idyllic nor ideal life style. It has its share of problems and frustrations. But if you enjoy people and if hard work doesn't scare you, it is a great career offering many pleasures and a deep sense of achievement.

Bonne chance!

EPILOGUE: ONE DAY IN THE LIFE OF A COUNTRY INNKEEPER

8:00 A.M.	Receive dairy and bread delivery
8:15 A.M.	Prepare coffee and donuts for inn guests
8:30 A.M.	Deliver breakfast trays to inn guests
8:45 A.M.	Innkeeper has breakfast
9:00 A.M.	Receive produce delivery; cook arrives
9:15 A.M. to 10:30 A.M.	Pay bills, answer correspondence, schedule employees; weekly payroll
10:30 A.M.	Order wines and beers
11:00 A.M.	Check out inn guests and supervise chambermaids
11:15 A.M.	Waitresses arrive
11:30 A.M. to 3:00 P.M.	Open café and gallery; serve lunch; supervise waitresses; register inn guests, cashier, help out where needed most, sell artwork and gifts; receptionist.
3:00 P.M.	Dishwasher arrives; prepare news releases, ads; register guests, cashier in art gallery; take break
4:00 P.M.	Dinner for innkeepers
4:30 P.M.	Cook arrives; receive deliveries as needed
5:30 P.M. to 8:30 P.M.	Waitresses arrive; open for dinner; same duties as during lunch service (11:30-3:00)
8:30 P.M.	Dinner service ends; dishwasher arrives; last dinner guests leave; cook and waitresses leave; shut off restaurant lights for night; plan next day's menu; place produce, bread, dairy orders for next day
10:30 P.M. to 11:30 P.M.	Closing tasks; tally of daily income figures
11:30 P.M.	Dishwasher leaves; lock doors; shut off lights
12:00 P.M.	(Get good night's sleep for next day!)

INDEX

INDEX

Accountant, 65, 66
Advertising, 32, 45, 114-16, 120, 122, 125, 128
Alcarese, Margie, 139, 140
Algonquin Hotel, 21, 43
Americana, 117
Ames, Jerry, 90
Analysis of potential sales, 74. *See also* Finances
Art gallery, 89, 90, 150, 151
Asa Ransom House, 25
Baileys, The 142
Banks, 63, 64. *See also* Mortgages, Finances
Barker, Ted and Marce, 24
Barley Sheaf Farm, 41
Barrows House, 26
Bathrooms, 47, 104, 105. *See also* Renovations, Redecorating
Beaumont Inn, 24, 117, 130

Bed and breakfast, 57
Bed and Breakfast Inn, 21, 96
Berkley, Kelley and Ashby, 25
Bernstein, Leo, 90
Bird and Bottle, 117
Blueberry Hill, 41, 56, 57
Board of Appeals, 69, 71, 72
Book list, 36-39
Boone Tavern, 130
Bramble, 41
Bramble Inn, The, 16, 43, 48, 54, 60, 67, 69, 71, 76, 78, 79, 81, 88, 89, 91-93, 107, 110, 112, 115, 116, 118, 123, 127, 130, 132, 151
Brazilian Court, 21
Breakfast, 141. *See also* Dining Room, Restaurant

INDEX

Brewster 1861 House, The, 49
Bride's Magazine, 54, 125
Britt House, 57, 90
Brochure, 114, 117-20
Brummer, Ed, 64, 112
Budget, 76, 147
Burch, Gregory, 60
Burn, The, 41, 90
Buxton Inn, The, 25, 88
Cancellation. *See* Reservations
Cape Cod Bramble, 129, 130
Cape Cod Guide, 81
Cape Cod Sea Camps, 79
Captain Lord Mansion, 96, 113, 117
Captain Whidbey Inn, 24, 91
Carrying costs, 41. *See also* Mortgage
Ceiling, 17
Chalet Suzanne, 91, 130
Chamber of Commerce, 44, 118, 122, 128
Charlotte Inn, 90, 94
Cheshire Inn, 55, 130
Chester Inn, 140
Christian Science Monitor, 117
Clark, Tony and Martha, 56
Clientele, 31, 43, 45, 46, 49, 55, 56, 116, 122, 133, 152
Colby Hill Inn, 60
Colonel Ebenezer Crafts Inn, 43
Common room, 47, 100, 101
Complaints, how to handle, 138, 139

Conover, Gery, 90
Consultant, 31, 64, 65
Conway, John Ashby, 35
Cookbook, 126, 130, 133. *See also* Promotion
Corcoran, Patricia, 60
Cornell School of Hotel Management, 34
Corporation, 67
Country Business Services, Inc., 32, 42, 55
Country Club Inn, 34
Country Inn, The, 34
Country Inns and Back Roads, 21, 77, 126, 127
Country Inns and Back Roads, Britain and Ireland, 127
Country Inns and Back Roads, Europe, 127
Credit cards, 144, 145
Crory, Bob and Sue, 34
Culinary Institute of America, 34
Cuttle's Mont Tremblant Club, 43
Darby Field Inn, 34, 35
Demographic study, 43, 44, 53
Deposit, 144. *See also* Reservations
Dewing, Ed and Jean, 35
Dickman, Chris, 90
Dining room, 30, 47, 57-59, 101, 102
Disaster file, 148, 149
Display ad, 119
Donaldson, Marc and Marily, 34

Index

Down payment, 31. *See also* Mortgage
Dream, 15, 23, 30
Durbin Hotel, 55
Durrast, Cora, 60
Early American Life, 117
Edge, Johnny and Betsi, 24
Elmwood Inn, 77
Embarrassing moments, 17, 57, 112, 139-42, 145
Energy-savings. *See* Insulation
Equipment. *See* Purchasing, Repairs
Existing business, 45
Expansion, 31, 47, 155, 156
Failure rate of businesses, 30
Fairfield Inn, 60
Farmhouse, The, 35, 78
Finances, 31-33, 51, 63-67, 72, 74, 75
Fire exits, 47
Food costs, 84-86. *See also* Purchasing
Formula for success, 155
"Freebies," 87
"Free Souvenirs," 154
Furnishings, 31, 95, 96. *See also* Shopping List
Gibson, Ken and Wendy, 34, 111
Gift shop, 152, 153
Gilbert, Bettie, 60
Glen Iris Inn, 54
Good will, 45, 46, 49
Goose Cove Lodge, 113
Graves Mountain Lodge, 81

Grey Rock Inn, 60
Grey Whale Inn, 54, 142
Gristmill Square, 34
Growth. *See* Expansion
Guest book, 148
Guido, Betsy, 140
Handfield Inn, 132
Harbor House, 54, 60
Harney, John, 34
Harper, Buzz and Bobbie, 90
Hawthorne Inn, 60
Hemlock Inn, 81
Heritage House, 43
Hickory Bridge Farm, 64, 78
Holmes, Brian, 79
Homestead, The, 54, 94, 96
Housing Inspection Service, 48
Hull, Bob and Fran, 26
Humor, 17
Hyde, Larry, 83, 138
Ideal guest profile, 55
Image, 46
Importing gift items, 153, 154
Income. *See* Finances
Independent Innkeepers Association, 126
Inn
 definition, 21
 name, 41, 42, 49
 size, 30
Inn at Huntington, 34, 132
Inn at Pleasant Hill, 130
Inn at Princeton, 56

163

Inn at Sawmill Farm, 25, 35, 94
Inn at Starlight Lake, 24, 117
Inn at Stone City, 96
Inn of the White Salmon, 91
Inn on the Library Lawn, 41, 83, 138
Inn on the Common, 96, 117
Innkeeper
  living quarters of, 47, 48
  as omnipresent, 112, 113
  personality of, 21, 22, 56, 57, 59, 60
  and reason to become, 23-25, 27, 28
  and relationship with guests, 138-42
  and rewards, 156
  and training, 34, 35
  typical day of, 27, 137, 138, 158
Innkeeping
  advance preparation for, 35-39
  authenticity of purpose, 55
  focus of, 40, 54-55
  as investment, 32-33
  needs leading to 23, 25, 26, 28, 29
  training for, 34-35
Inspections, fire and health, 71
Insulation, 32
Insurance, 31, 66
Inventory, 107
Inverary Inn, 25

James House, 57
Jamieson House, 56
Jared Coffin House, 64
Jefferson Hotel, 21
Kitchen, 47, 67, 84, 102, 103. *See also* Restaurant
Koppeis, Frank, 67
Landscaping, 31, 48
Laundry room, 105
Lawyer, 65, 66
Leger, Connie, 91
Lenz, Judy and Bob, 25
Licenses, 31, 68, 70
Life style, 15, 18, 25, 26, 157
Limited partnership, 67
Lincklaen House, 60
Lincoln, Joseph, 41
Location, 40-44, 46-48, 54, 91, 126, 155
Lodge on the Desert, 55, 132
Lodging bedrooms, 30, 103, 104. *See also* Redecorating, Reservations
Logo, 115, 118, 120
Longfellow's Wayside Inn, 67, 88
Lowell Inn, 24, 94
Lyme Inn, 94
MacAulay, Scott, 25
Magazines, 117, 120, 122. *See also* Advertising
Mailing list, 148
Mainstay Inn, 54, 126.
Maintenance, 47, 146, 147. *See also* Repairs
Marathon Hotel, 54

Index

Martin, Daun and Robert, 90
Maryland Inn, 132
McBroom, Theodora and Bruce, 35
McMahon Family, 24
McWilliams, Jack, 34
Menu, 59, 79-81
Millet, Janet, 60
"Mom and Pop" business, 25
Mortgage, 33, 41, 63, 64. *See also* Finances
Moyse, Nora McNab, 130
Murphy's Law, 17, 98
National Historic Trust, 67
National House, The, 54, 64, 126
Nauset House Inn, 54, 125
New England Hotel, Motel, and Restaurant Trade Show, 79
New York Times Manual of Home Repairs, 27
New Yorker, 117
Newspapers, 116, 117, 119, 123, 125. *See also* Advertising
News release, 123-25, 132-33. *See also* Advertising
North, Bill, 34
Nu-Wray Inn, 60, 81, 130
Old Milano Hotel, 35
Old Rittenhouse Inn, 54, 56, 132
One day in the life of innkeeper, 158

Opening day, 16, 116
Opinicon, The, 41
Orr, Audrey and Orville, 25
Outlook Lodge, 54
Ownership, forms of business, 66, 67
Palmer, Maureen and Arthur, 24
Parking spaces, 46, 58, 84
Partnerships, 67
Partridge Inn, 81, 130
Pasquaney Inn, 35
Patchwork Quilt Inn, 94
Pearson, Paul, 132
Pentagoet Inn, 60, 81
Permits, 46, 68, 69
Personal hospitality, 146
Personal involvement, 22
Personnel, 44, 45, 59, 83, 84, 88, 109-13, 116
Pets, 142
Philbrook Farm Inn, 64, 91
Philbrook, Nancy, 91
Pine Crest Inn, 26
Plumbing, 27. *See also* Repairs
Purchasing
  cash discounts, 98
  equipment and supplies, 97, 99-106
  food, 106
  helpful hints, 108
  wine, beer, alcohol, 107, 108
Public hearings, 69
Public relations, 125
Publicity, 90, 114, 123, 126

165

INDEX

Product development, 129-31. *See also* Promotion
Pro forma Analysis, 72, 73, 75, 76, 87
Promotion, 114, 116, 128-33
Pump House Inn, 117
Radio, 120, 121, 128. *See also* Advertising
"Rat-race," 26, 156
Read, Philip and Peggy, 64
Real estate, 32, 33
Real estate trust, 67
Reception area, 94, 100
Record-keeping, 99, 147-49
Red Castle Inn, 90
Redcoat's Return, 41, 140
Redecorating, 92-96. *See also* Renovations, Restoration
Red Inn, 24, 78
Reed, Suzanne, 56
Renovations, 31, 48, 49, 146. *See also* Redecorating, Restoration, Repairs
Repairs, 16, 17, 31, 98, 99, 138. *See also* Maintenance
Research, 47
Reservations, 143, 144
Restaurant, 77, 78, 82-86. *See also* Dining Room as live theater, 87, 88
Restoration, 31, 126. *See also* Renovations, Redecoration

Richardson's Canal House Inn, 78
Riverside Inn, 25, 81, 88
Robert Morris Inn, 34, 111
Rockhouse Mountain Farm, 24, 41
Saunders, Natalie, 60
Schubert, Marilyn and Charles, 26
Schumacher, Nancy and John, 25
Schumacher's New Prague Hotel, 25, 91
Schuman, Murray, 34
Seasonal business, 30, 49-52, 76
Seating capacity, 58, 84
Service Corps of Retired Executives (SCORE), 39
Service mark, 131
"Service with a smile," 145, 146
1740 House, The, 117
Shaw, Gordon, 24
Shaw's Hotel, 24, 64
Shipe, Mary Jo and Jim, 35
Shopping list, 100-6
Signs, 31, 46, 71
Silvermine Tavern, 24
Simpson, Norman, 13, 126, 127
Sinervo, Walter, 79
Single proprietorship, 66, 67
Sjogren, Elizabeth, 56
Small Business Association (SBA), 35-38, 79

166

Index

Small Business Reporter, 39
Smith, Janice and Stafford, 35
Smithsonian, 117
Spaulding Inn Club, 54
Special events. *See* Promotion
Special permit, 69, 70
Spirit of innkeeping, 157
Stafford's Bay View, 35
Stafford's in the Field, 132
Stone, John, 24
Stone, Steve and Shirlie, 24
Subchapter S corporation, 67
Success, 22, 31, 43, 46, 155, 157
Suppliers, 44, 45. *See also* Equipment
Sutter Creek Inn, 60
Taber, Gladys, 42
Tavern, The, 60
Tax advantages, 33
Television, 127, 128
Theme, 40, 89, 90-91, 150
and color, 93-94
Thomas, David, 60
Tobin, Helen, 60
Toll House Inn, 129
Town Farms Inn, 77
Trademarks, 131
Trade organizations, 128, 129. *See also* Promotion
Traffic flow, 47, 48, 93
Training, 34-35
Travel guide books, 39, 126, 127
Trends in Hotel Business, 39
"Turnover," 75, 82
Undercapitalization, 30
Union Street Hotel, 21
Variances, 69, 70
Visual recognition, 118
Volume, 82. *See also* Restaurant
Warranty, 99, 149
Waterford Inne, The, 94
Way, Jane, 60
Wayside Inn, 90, 139
Welshfield Inn, 78, 79
Whistling Oyster, 41, 78
White Gull Inn, 81
White Hart Inn, 34
Whitehall Inn, 35, 117
Whitman, Frank, 24
Williams, Brill, 25
Williams, Rod and Ione, 35
Windsor House, 57
Wine Country Inn, 43
Woodbound Inn, 64, 65, 112
Working capital, 31
Wray, Rush, 60
Wright, Peggy and Tom, 141, 142
Zoning, 46, 48, 58, 69, 71, 72. *See also* Location